REAL Teachers, REAL Challenges, REAL Solutions

25 Ways to Handle the Challenges of the Classroom Effectively

Annette L. Breaux
and
Elizabeth Breaux

EYE ON EDUCATION

6 DEPOT WAY WEST, SUITE 106

LARCHMONT, NY 10538

(914) 833–0551

(914) 833–0761 fax

www.eyeoneducation.com

Library of Congress Cataloging-in-Publication Data

Breaux, Annette L.
    Real teachers, real challenges, real solutions : 25 ways to handle the challenges of the classroom effectively / Annette L. Breaux and Elizabeth Breaux.
        p.   cm.
    ISBN 1-930556-64-0
    1. Classroom management—Handbooks, manuals, etc. 2. Teacher effectiveness—Handbooks, manuals, etc. I. Breaux, Elizabeth, 1961– II. Title.

    LB3013.B67 2004
    371.102′4–dc21

                                                                            2003053162

10 9 8 7 6 5

Editorial and production services provided by
Richard H. Adin Freelance Editorial Services
52 Oakwood Blvd., Poughkeepsie, NY 12603-4112
(845-471-3566)

Also Available from EYE ON EDUCATION

101 "Answers" for New Teachers and Their Mentors:
Effective Teaching Tips for Daily Classroom Use
Annette L. Breaux

Coaching and Mentoring
First-Year and Student Teachers
India J. Podsen and Vicki Denmark

Teacher Retention:
What Is Your Weakest Link?
India J. Podsen

The Principal as Instructional Leader:
A Handbook for Supervisors
Sally J. Zepeda

Handbook on Teacher Portfolios for Evaluation
and Professional Development (Includes CD-ROM)
Pamela Tucker, James Strong, and Christopher Gareis

Motivating and Inspiring Teachers:
The Educator's Guide for Building Staff Morale
Todd Whitaker, Beth Whitaker, and Dale Lumpa

Teaching Matters:
Motivating & Inspiring Yourself
Todd and Beth Whitaker

Dealing with Difficult Teachers, Second Edition
Todd Whitaker

Staff Development: Practices That
Promote Leadership in Learning Communities
Sally J. Zepeda

The Call to Teacher Leadership
Sally J. Zepeda

Differentiated Instruction:
A Guide for Elementary School Teachers
Amy Benjamin

Differentiated Instruction:
A Guide for Middle and High School Teachers
Amy Benjamin

*We gratefully dedicate this book
to our parents, with love.*

About the Authors

Annette Breaux is one of the most entertaining and informative authors and speakers in education. She leaves her audiences with practical techniques to implement in their classrooms immediately. Administrators agree that they see results from teachers instantly.

Her message is one of practicality and personality in teaching, of feeling and healing in touching students' lives, and of common sense and creative teaching strategies. Her writings and presentations generate instant impact on the relationships between teachers and students.

A curriculum coordinator and former classroom teacher, she is also the director of the FIRST Program, an induction program for new teachers hailed as one of the best in the country. The program has been adopted by the Louisiana Department of Education as a statewide model. Annette is the author of "101 Answers for New Teachers and their Mentors" and the coauthor, with Dr. Harry K. Wong, of "New Teacher Induction: How to Train, Support, and Retain New Teachers."

Elizabeth Breaux is a speaker who leaves her audiences crying, laughing, and certain that they have chosen the right profession—teaching. She captivates her audiences by sharing with them the real-life experiences of reaching and teaching students of all academic levels and from all walks of life.

Her message is a simple one: "I cannot teach my students until I reach my students." She has taught "at-risk" students for the past eighteen years and has enjoyed phenomenal success.

A master teacher, Elizabeth now serves as a curriculum coordinator in Lafayette, Louisiana.

Annette and Elizabeth, affectionately referred to as "Sister Act" by their audiences, are a truly dynamic duo. Their down-south warmth, infectious humor, and ability to touch the hearts and souls of educators invariably bring audiences to their feet. Teachers who have read their writings or heard them speak agree that they walk away with user-friendly information, heartfelt inspiration, and a much-needed reminder that they truly have chosen the most noble of all professions—teaching.

Foreword

Our reasons for writing this book are twofold: (1) to improve the quality of teaching and learning, and (2) to ease the way for teachers in dealing with the challenges of the classroom. In every school, in every classroom, for every teacher, there are challenges. In every school, in every classroom, for every student, there are challenges. In every school, in every classroom, for every teacher and student, it is far more productive to focus not on struggling with challenges, but rather on finding solutions that foster growth.

Thus, throughout the book, you will read about situations involving *real* teachers, *real* challenges, and *real* solutions. You will notice that nothing we suggest or discuss relates, in any way, to fads or trends or innovations or the latest "whatevers" in education. Regardless of whom you teach, where you teach, or what you teach, the basic principles of good teaching shared in this book will apply to *you*.

As teachers, we share a sense of camaraderie based on our common purpose—the desire to make a difference. It is our sincere desire and privilege to assist you in becoming the best teacher that you can possibly be. The children—we are all here for the children. Let us not forget or take lightly our responsibility to the children. They are our future.

If you benefit from this book, then, too, will your students. Indeed, together, we will have all touched the future with our influence.

Annette and Elizabeth Breaux

Table of Contents

Introduction

What We Believe

- We believe that students come to us with a keen awareness of who they are and who they are not.

- We believe that it is our job, as teachers, to awaken each student's underlying potential.

- We believe that truly effective teaching is twofold. It requires, first, that the desired outcome be achieved, and secondly that it be achieved through methods that are effective for both the students and the teacher. We believe that both of these factors are critical to the development of the student—academically and socially.

- We believe that every student—*every* student—deserves a quality education.

- We believe that the quality of the education that a child receives in school hinges upon the quality of the classroom teacher.

- We believe that teachers can and do touch lives.

- We believe that *every* student is worthwhile, unique, special, teachable, and reachable.

Common Teacher Challenges

From our daily dealings with teachers and students across the country, along with our own experiences in the classroom, we have compiled what we have found to be some of the most common classroom challenges and have provided techniques and suggestions for handling these challenges efficiently, effectively, and appropriately.

How to Use this Book

This book is filled with examples of typical classroom scenarios, along with both an effective and an ineffective way to handle each. You will enjoy reading it either from cover to cover, section by section, or skipping around to suit your immediate needs.

However you choose to read this book, rest assured that you will recognize yourself and your coworkers on many of its pages. The scenarios are real and were taken from the real-life experiences of teachers just like you.

Don't forget to laugh enthusiastically when you find yourself in the midst of these pages! It is only when we can laugh at our own mistakes that we can grow as professionals. Also, it's only when we're able to laugh at ourselves that others can tolerate us! Show us a teacher who cannot have a good laugh at himself, and we'll show you a miserable person with a classroom of miserable students!

What This Book Will Do For You

- ♦ If you are searching for simple, basic, common-sense answers to common teacher challenges,
- ♦ If you are an effective teacher seeking to become even more effective,
- ♦ If you are committed to becoming the teacher that every student wants and deserves,
- ♦ If you believe in treating your students with professionalism and dignity,
- ♦ If you struggle, as do all good teachers, with daily classroom challenges, and
- ♦ If you are a committed, dedicated individual who truly aspires to touching lives and making a difference,

... then this book is for you. Enjoy!

Dealing with Students

A student comes to me
A soiled dove with heavy wings
Flailing aimlessly
Angry at everything and everyone
At nothing and no one
Rejected, ridiculed, misunderstood
Hurting, injured, waiting to be healed
I must first reach him and pull him in
Before I can teach him to fly again.

Elizabeth Breaux

*FACT: If you **tell** a student what you want, **show** him exactly how to do it, **practice** with him how to do it, and **praise** him when he succeeds, then the chances of his actually **doing** it increase a hundredfold!*

Getting Students to Do What You Want Them to Do

Classroom Scenario

A group of students goes to teacher "one." In teacher "one's" classroom the students talk and talk and the teacher fusses and fusses. The more they talk, the more she fusses. During transitions, the students roam freely about the classroom and the teacher fusses more. Several names go up on the board followed by protests from the "named" ones that the others were talking also. One student is sent to the office because he will not get busy doing his work. The "lesson" goes on as the teacher lectures over the students' talking. She stops only for the occasional "warning." She calls on students who are not paying attention and, of course, they cannot answer the content-related questions. These students are then reprimanded for not paying attention. One student asks to go the restroom and the teacher allows her to go. Another then asks to go to the restroom and the teacher says, "You just want to go because I let someone else go. Now sit down and be quiet." One student walks up to the pencil sharpener and two more quickly follow. A lengthy discussion (that appears quite interesting) ensues. The teacher warns them to hurry with their sharpening and be seated. As soon as they are seated, two more students decide that a discussion at the pencil sharpener seems inviting, so they pursue it. Okay, you get the picture. Now on to teacher "two's" classroom...

The bell rings, and the same group of students chaotically leaves the classroom of teacher "one." As the students approach the classroom doorway of teacher "two," something magical occurs! It has to be magic. There's no other explanation. *Or is there?* The students walk into the classroom and are greeted by the teacher at the doorway. They do this in an orderly fashion. As each student enters, he immediately sits in his desk and gets busy doing the bellwork assignment that is posted on the board. The teacher enters and holds her hand up, smiling quietly. All students quickly return the gesture. This is the "signal" for all eyes on the teacher and quiet. The teacher thanks the students for following the procedure and announces that they have one minute to complete the bellwork. (During this time, the teacher efficiently checks the roll.) The students eagerly complete the assignment and a meaningful, organized discussion takes place. The bellwork leads into the day's lesson, and the teacher's enthusiasm for the lesson is contagious. The lesson flows smoothly and students eagerly participate. There are structured procedures, which all students follow—procedures for getting quiet; procedures for getting the teacher's attention; procedures for pencil sharpening; procedures for working cooperatively with others; procedures for both entering and exiting the classroom; procedures for passing in papers; and on and on and on. It seems as though even the procedures have procedures! The same "chaotic" students from teacher "one's" classroom have been "magically" transformed into productive learners in a well-organized environment. There is no complaining, there are no threats, there is no bickering. There is learning going on, and it's happening in a structured way! The teacher and the students are happy and successful!

What's Effective

Obviously, what teacher "two" is doing is effective. So let's analyze that. Notice that this teacher has a definite, highly structured classroom management plan in place. The procedures have been practiced and reinforced so many times that they have now become "routines." The students know what to do, and they do it. In fact they do it so well that the classroom hums like a well-rehearsed church choir! You see, the key is structure. Students need structure. And when structured procedures are in place, there are very few discipline problems. To obtain this type of structure, you, the teacher, must set the procedures, model them, practice them with the students—again and again and again—and then reinforce as necessary. You don't "punish" when a student forgets the procedure. You simply practice the procedure again. Fairly soon, they get so tired of practicing that they just follow the darned procedure in order not to practice it yet again! It works like a charm. But *you* must remain consistent. Procedures are consistent ways of doing things. So you can't set a procedure and then forget about it. Once you set it, that's it. That's the way it will be done every single time, every single day.

What's *Not* Effective

Though it goes without saying that what teacher "one" is doing is not effective, let's say it anyway: "What teacher one is doing is not effective!" Admit it, teachers. We all do it. We "expect" sometimes that students just "know" what to do or what they should do. And then when they don't do what we expect, we become outdone and indignant. So we fuss. And then we fuss some more. We punish, we threaten, we beg and plead, we dare students to misbehave, we sigh, we growl, and whatever else imaginable that causes us to lose our professionalism. But it never works. If it did, we wouldn't be fussing anymore. And if you're doing what teacher "one" was doing, you're still fussing! If you don't set procedures, the students will create their own. And hats off to our students' creative abilities in setting their own procedures. However, remember that procedures are "consistent" ways of doing things—not creative ways of doing things!

Bottom Line

How can we expect students to know what we want them to do if we don't tell them *exactly* what we expect, show them how to do what we want them to do, practice the consistent way to do a certain thing, and then reinforce when necessary? Students need direction. They are not mind readers! And we can all be grateful for that fact, because if they could read our minds in the classroom, they wouldn't always like us very much!

Does it make sense to teach students to learn a language, use it appropriately, think deeply, and solve problems in silence?

Managing Student Talking

Classroom Scenario

Said Mr. Dennis, "I'm in control in my classroom. Students speak when spoken to. You won't walk past my classroom and hear any noise unless it's coming from *me*. My students know that I insist upon quiet." And he was right. Upon entering his classroom, students were "greeted" with a scowl from Mr. Dennis. He was tall in stature and short on words. The silence in his classroom was deafening. Mr. Dennis was the most feared and dreaded teacher in the school. Each day, he doled out the day's lesson in his "oh so quiet and threatening" tone. And then the students "got busy" completing worksheets and writing paragraphs and reading his "loudly *red*" comments on their papers. There was no active participation, no student talking, no collaboration, and no noise! It was just as Mr. Dennis liked it.

The office never heard from Mr. Dennis, as he had no discipline problems. He literally "scared" his students silent. Oddly enough, at the end of the school year, his students inevitably scored low, both on their report cards and on the district's criterion-referenced test in English. Mr. Dennis had the perfect justification every year: "Students today just don't care. Neither do their parents. If they can't learn English in my classroom, they won't learn it anywhere. But I'll keep drilling it into them, whether they like it or not."

What's Effective

After reading about Mr. Dennis, you may be tempted to skip ahead to "What's *Not* Effective," because if you are an effective teacher, then you know that Mr. Dennis typifies what is not effective. But be patient. We'll get to him in a minute. First, consider this: If you were learning a language, could you do it in silence?—of course not. In an effective classroom, regardless of what subject you teach, unless, of course, you are teaching spies to remain silent under torture, silence is not the norm. But let's be clear on the difference between "inappropriate noise" and "constructive noise." Inappropriate noise occurs in the classrooms of teachers lacking in classroom management skills. In these classrooms there is no order to the noise. Students are engaged in casual conversations completely unrelated to the subject matter. The teachers in these classrooms are usually adding to that noise by begging, pleading with, and threatening the students. This type of "noise" is not effective. Okay, so what *is* effective? In the classroom of an effective teacher, students actually do most of the talking. They are constantly involved, either in discussions with the teacher or in structured discussions with one another. There is rarely a silent moment in the classroom of an effective teacher, aside from students taking a test or completing a task independently. Cooperative grouping is the norm in these classrooms. These classrooms are "exciting" places. You see, it is virtually impossible to have a silent environment that is exciting. In the exciting classroom, of course, noise levels are controlled so as not to be distracting. Again, structure is the key.

What's *Not* Effective

 Two things are not effective: (1) silent classrooms, and (2) classrooms with unstructured noise. In the case of Mr. Dennis, his classroom was the "oh, too typical silent classroom." Yes, the environment was controlled all right, so much so that learning could not take place effectively. And to think that he was teaching a language, English, and was attempting to do it in silence! In a classroom buzzing with unstructured noise, teachers are usually too busy fussing about the noise to be able to teach effectively. Fussing, by the way, falls into the category of unstructured noise.

Bottom Line

 Gone are the days of the silent classroom. And gone they should be! Silence is not golden in the classroom. If children are seen and not heard in the classroom, then children are not learning in the classroom. Active classrooms where students talk together, think aloud, and work cooperatively and collaboratively are not silent places. Walk into the classroom of an effective teacher. You'll "see" the excitement, you'll "feel" the excitement, and yes, you will "hear" the excitement. To put it succinctly,

> *Noise is golden when children are heard*
> *Excitement exuding from each spoken word*
> *Questioning everything as children do*
> *Uncovering answers, discovering what's new*
> *And oh so joyful to play some small part*
> *I teach the children, I touch the heart!*
>
> Annette L. Breaux

FACT 1: Students will get distracted. It's called "off task" behavior.

FACT 2: The more time students spend "on task," the higher their achievement.

FACT 3: There are both effective and ineffective ways of dealing with "off task" behavior.

FACT 4: The effective ways work—the ineffective ways don't.

Dealing with Off-Task Behavior

Classroom Scenario

In a typical classroom on a typical day, students tend to get off task by daydreaming, talking to one another, writing notes to one another, and just not paying attention for whatever reason. We will take a look into the classrooms of two teachers, Ms. Proactive (Ms. P) and Ms. Reactive (Ms. R). It is the first week of school. Both are teaching the same students. Both face the challenges of dealing with off-task behavior. One deals with the challenges effectively and "nips them in the bud." The other deals with the same challenges ineffectively and allows them to escalate into full-blown problems. Follow us, first, into the classroom of Ms. P.

What's Effective

 Ms. P is holding a discussion with her class. During the discussion, she notices that Timothy is "far away" inside of a daydream. She continues the discussion and moves closer to Timothy. There is no change in her tone, no change in the manner in which the discussion is being held. She simply moves closer to Timothy. As she reaches his desk, she stands there, still continuing with the discussion. Timothy immediately snaps out of his daydream and joins the world of the classroom. He is back on task. The discussion continues and Ms. P notices that Susan is attempting to get the attention of Natasha so that she can pass along a note. Ms. P stops the discussion and says, "Susan." Susan thinks that she is "busted" and she stops dead in her tracks. Ms. P simply smiles and says, "Remind me that I have to tell you something before you leave today. I'm afraid I'll forget, so please remind me if I do." Susan nods and breathes a sigh of relief. She then puts the note away. Has she been "busted?" She's not sure, but she's definitely back on task. And by the way, Ms. P has no idea what she's going to tell Susan, as it was just a clever way of getting her back on task. But she's a teacher. She'll think of something!

Following the discussion, students spend a few minutes on a written assignment. Ms. P notices that Fred is doing nothing. Everyone else is working, but Fred is simply sitting in his desk, staring into space. Ms. P walks over to Fred and quietly says, "As soon as you finish, let me know. I need to ask a favor of you when you finish. Since Fred is hoping that he'll be able to run an errand (something that all students love to do), he immediately gets started. Upon finishing, he proudly displays his work for Ms. P and she then asks him to help her move a small table from the back of the room to the front of the room. He is more than happy to help.

Some time later, the bell rings signaling the end of the period. The students now walk next door to the classroom of Ms. R. Same students, same challenges, different results. Let's see why things go awry.

What's *Not* Effective

 The class has begun, and Ms. R is holding a discussion with the students. Since Timothy did not get a chance to finish his daydream in Ms. P's class, he revisits it in Ms. R's class. Noticing that Timothy is "far away," Ms. P stops the discussion and stares at Timothy. A silence falls upon the class and Timothy is awakened by the silence only to feel the heat of Ms. R's glare. Ms. R then says, in a tone that more than hints at sarcasm, "Well, Timothy, I'm so glad that you decided to join us." Timothy gets defensive and insists that he *was* paying attention. Determined to prove herself "right," Ms. R then proceeds to question him about what has just been discussed. Timothy, of course, cannot come up the correct answers. This makes him angrier, and a power struggle ensues. He is determined now to "get her back." Maybe today, maybe later, but he'll "get her" for embarrassing him in front of his peers.... He pouts for the remainder of the class period and is completely removed from anything that is going on in class. As the discussion continues, Susan remembers that she still has the note for Natasha. She attempts to get Natasha's attention by waving the note in her hand. Ms. R marches straight to Susan and pulls the note from her hand. Again, another power struggle ensues. Susan decides to talk to Timothy after class. Maybe they can commiserate and cooperate in their master plan to "get back" at Ms. R. Susan, too, has been lost for the remainder of the class period.

As students are later completing a task at their desks, Fred, as is his tendency, is doing nothing. Ms. R tells him in no uncertain terms that he had better get busy if he wants to avoid after-school detention. Fred continues to do nothing. She warns him again, and he says he doesn't understand what he's supposed to do. Ms. R continues to threaten him, and soon he is sent to the office for willful disobedience. Susan adds his name to the list for commiseration and cooperation. There's power in numbers!

Bottom Line

Off-task behavior is common. It's normal. It's inevitable. Therefore, you, the teacher, have a choice. You can deal with the challenges in a "proactive" manner or in a "reactive" manner. If you deal with them in a proactive manner by "nipping them in the bud" before they escalate into real problems, your approaches will be effective. If you deal with them in a reactive manner by acting out of emotions, taking the behaviors personally, and daring students to continue the behaviors, your approaches will be ineffective.

Ms. P deals with the challenges effectively. As a result, she gets the three off-task students back on task. At the same time, she maintains their dignity. She's off to a great start because she knows how to keep students on task. Thus, her students will achieve, which will make for a wonderful and productive school year!

Ms. R deals with the challenges ineffectively. As a result, she loses the three off-task students. She does this by compromising their dignity and thus inviting revenge. This is only the first week of school. Both she and her students have entered the boxing ring. The students are determined to be victorious, hoping for a "knock-out" before the fifteenth round! Ding!

I didn't understand, but my teacher just moved on
She said she had no time to wait for the light on me to dawn
So on she moved and there I stayed; she left me in the dust
The idea that I was capable was one she did not trust
How far would I have gone had she given me her all,
Had she reached out her hand to me and not just let me fall
I guess I'll never really know, but I know it's not too late
I have a brand new teacher now who has not sealed my fate
She says that I can do it; we work until I do
She's patient and determined. She believes in me. Do you?

Annette L. Breaux

Getting Students to Understand Concepts

Classroom Scenario

Teacher A: "It's time to move on to division, and some of my students still do not understand multiplication! But I can't wait for them. I've got to move on."

Teacher B: "How can you move on when they don't yet understand?"

Teacher A: "Look, I've got to cover the textbook, and I'm already behind. If I don't move on, I'll never get the material covered."

Teacher B: "But if you move on, they won't understand division either. Then you'll really lose them."

Teacher A: "That's their problem. Maybe if they'd study more, they'd get it. But the fact that they don't is not my fault. And by the way, you're teaching the same grade level as I. Have you gotten to division yet?"

Teacher B: "Yes, actually, we're well into division right now."

Teacher A: "So what did you do with the ones who didn't understand multiplication?"

Teacher B: "They all understand multiplication. I couldn't have moved on to division if they didn't."

Teacher A: "Well, you're just lucky to have gotten the students who understand. I, on the other hand, always seem to get the students who don't!"

What's Effective

A closer look into each of these two classrooms revealed that the students were really no different in either classroom regarding their abilities. However, they were quite different with regard to their achievement levels. This same close look into these classrooms revealed that the main difference was the teaching! Surprised? In order to look at what's effective, we will look to Teacher B. In Teacher B's classroom, this is what we saw:

♦ Enthusiasm on the part of the teacher
♦ Enthusiasm on the part of the students
♦ A belief that all students could and would succeed
♦ Exciting, student-centered lessons
♦ Lots of structured student talking
♦ Remediation for those students who did not understand
♦ Enrichment for those students who did understand
♦ Organization
♦ Well-planned lessons
♦ Excellent classroom management
♦ A positive, inviting, engaging atmosphere
♦ Happy, successful students!

What's *Not* Effective

Yep. You guessed it. A look into Teacher A's classroom will reveal precisely what you are expecting—the exact opposite of what we saw in the classroom of Teacher B. Suffer along with us as we take a look into the classroom of Teacher A:

♦ Lack of enthusiasm on the part of the teacher
♦ Lack of enthusiasm on the part of the students
♦ A belief that many students could not and would not succeed

- Boring, teacher-centered lessons
- Lots of unstructured student talking—having nothing to do with the lessons
- No remediation for students who did not understand
- No enrichment for students who did understand
- Lack of organization
- Poorly-planned lessons
- Lack of any system of classroom management
- A negative, uninviting, disengaging atmosphere
- Unhappy, unsuccessful students!

Bottom Line

 The absolute bottom line is this: Any student can be successful in the hands of an effective teacher. Effective teachers do whatever it takes to ensure that concepts are well-taught and thoroughly understood. They simply do not settle for anything less.

You see, it is the TEACHER who makes the difference in the classroom, just as it is the surgeon who makes the difference in the operating room, just as it is the mechanic who makes the difference in the way the engine runs, just as it is the architect who makes the difference in the structure of a building, just as it is the cook who makes the difference in the kitchen! An effective cook can take potted meat and turn it into a delicacy. An ineffective cook can take a 3-inch filet mignon and turn it into something that even the dog won't eat. Do what's effective. Do what's best for your students. Do the things that make the difference in the classroom. Be a Teacher B. Do it, and do it now. The children cannot wait!

> ### Lost Within a Shout
>
> *You yelled at me and I yelled back*
> *What else was there to do?*
> *We yelled some more, our throats got sore*
> *And the tension grew and grew*
> *And finally, in exhaustion, we both ran out of steam*
> *Left standing in embarrassment, no pride left to redeem*
> *What point is there in thinking that being "right" we must*
> *And pushing on till all involved just lose respect and trust?*
> *Maybe if we'd listened, we could have met half way*
> *Let's talk next time and really hear what the other has to say*
> *For if we both could do that, maybe we'd find out*
> *That never has a point been made when lost within a shout!*
>
> Annette L. Breaux

Dealing with Disrespectful Student Behaviors

Classroom Scenario

It was the first day of school and in walked Albert Wilson. Albert was almost sixteen years old and in the seventh grade. Albert had an agenda: He would make certain that his teachers knew not to *mess with him!* He would soon be quitting school and had no intentions of doing anything until then, other than biding his time. The teachers were to simply leave him alone. Expecting anything from him would be a mistake on their parts. His intention was (should anyone forget this) to be a constant reminder of that fact.

Albert was in for a big surprise, however, when he met his math teacher, Diane Adams. What Albert didn't know was that Ms. Adams had many years of experience and practice in dealing with the challenges of reaching

◆ 19

and teaching the many "Albert Wilsons" of the world. Ms. Adams obviously understood the concept of "approach being everything" when she was faced with her first challenge from Albert.

As Ms. Adams walked around the room providing assistance to her students, she approached the vicinity of Albert's desk. As she got closer, she noticed Albert staring directly at her with his pencil held firmly by both hands. As Ms. Adams approached Albert's desk, Albert held the pencil high, angrily snapping it in two.

What's Effective

 Being a seasoned veteran, Ms. Adams was accustomed to dealing immediately with a situation that requires the perfect approach. Needing a few seconds to devise a "plan of action," Ms. Adams intuitively "bought some time" by calmly turning and walking away from Albert.

Diane Adams chose to be the consummate professional, despite the fact that Albert Wilson had just been utterly disrespectful to her. She simply walked over to her can of old, used pencils, (the short ones with very little eraser left on them), picked one from the can, and handed it to Albert. She let him know that, first, she understood his frustration. In the future, however, should he feel the need to snap a pencil, he should simply alert her so that she could give him one of the old pencils to break. She explained to him that she would like to keep the newer ones for his and other students' use in the classroom.

By using this approach, Ms. Adams became an excellent model for Albert, and other students, of how to appropriately handle a situation where emotions can sometimes take over our better judgment.

Ms. Adams chose to place Albert's future success in her class ahead of her own need to attempt to "win" in a situation where everyone can potentially lose. Not only did she manage to defuse what could have been a very volatile situation, but she made a lifesaving choice concerning the future of Albert Wilson. Albert did not quit school. In fact, he finished the year and moved on to high school. He also came to trust Ms. Adams with academic and personal issues as the year progressed. And though he may have broken several pencil points while diligently doing his work, he *never* broke a pencil in anger again!

What's *Not* Effective

Unfortunately, effectively dealing with tough situations on the spur of the moment is a skill that stems from experience *and* from the proper attitude. Ms. Adams obviously possessed the skill of managing her own reactions to tough situations.

Had she not displayed the necessary restraint, she may simply have allowed her emotions to rule her reactions, thereby ensuring that Albert would remain a victim of himself, and she a victim of Albert.

Ms. Adams could have chosen to display the same reaction to frustration as did Albert. She could have added fuel to the fire (that Albert had managed to spark) by allowing herself to be reduced to the level where emotions rule. She could have yelled at Albert, pointing out how disrespectful and rude he was being (which, of course, were his intentions to begin with). She could have ordered him out of the room, to the office, or chosen some other familiar course of action to which less effective teachers are accustomed.

Bottom Line

♦ It takes one person to be disrespectful. It takes two people to turn it into a power struggle.

♦ True professionals do not engage in power struggles. Instead, they defuse them.

♦ Effective teachers do not take disrespect personally. They recognize the frustration of the student, they think through their reactions to the student, and then they act in a professional manner.

♦ Once a student knows that you are on his "side" as opposed to being "out to get him," he will stop trying to get *you*!

♦ Even the "hardest" hearts can be softened with the right approach! Effective teachers realize this, and they use it to their advantage, and ultimately, to the advantage of the students.

♦ In win-win situations, no one loses! Okay, maybe that's overstating the obvious.... Turn every potential negative situation into one that fosters growth, that maintains dignity, and that speaks only of professionalism!

♦ *Remember*: When dealing with any type of student misbehavior, and when dealing with anyone, "approach is everything!"

> *I didn't do my homework, and my teacher's really mad*
> *Not about my homework, but the lousy excuse I had*
> *It started when I left my books inside my desk again*
> *And instead of telling Mom the truth, I blamed it on my friend*
> *I told her that my friend had brought my books home by mistake*
> *But since I had no homework, no difference would it make*
> *So now my teacher asks for it, and again I tell a lie*
> *One lie breeds another—there's no stopping it, I've tried!*
> *"My mom is in the hospital, my dad was working late,*
> *I had to watch the baby, so my homework had to wait."*
> *She asks me if I realize that she wasn't born today*
> *She saw my mom this morning, and so much she had to say…*
> *She said my mom was feeling fine, and my dad's been home for days*
> *And my books are right there in my desk where I left them yesterday!*
>
> Elizabeth Breaux

Getting Students to Complete Homework Assignments

Classroom Scenario

Maria, yet again, does not have her homework. This has happened several times. Maria is one of those students who just doesn't seem to be able to bring in her homework assignments. Oh, yes, she is capable of doing the work, as are most students who do not bring in assignments. And yes, her home life leaves much to be desired, but that does not relieve her from her responsibilities. Mr. Harris must deal with this problem. He has tried several approaches, including changing his homework assignments so that they are more interesting. He does not overload his students with homework, as he believes that *he* is responsible for teaching the students in class. Homework is occasionally assigned, however, for reinforcement purposes, and it is expected that all students complete these assignments in a timely fashion. Almost all of his students do turn in their assignments, so he knows that he must deal with this problem on an individual basis.

Mr. Harris decides to apply his knowledge of psychology with Maria. He realizes, as all teachers do, that almost without exception, students—all students of all age levels, ability levels, motivation levels, etc.—love to run errands for the teacher. He decides to make this knowledge work for him, and, ultimately, for Maria. Here's what he does:

Mr. Harris approaches Maria and says, "Look, Maria, I know that you're upset with yourself for not turning in your homework assignment. (This is a stretch. Maria never seems to care much when she does not turn in her assignments. But stay with us and watch where he is heading.) "Please don't be too hard on yourself. I have no doubt that you'll have your assignment tomorrow. Oh, and by the way, I need for you to run an errand for me tomorrow, but I'm afraid I'll forget about it. Please write a note on the top of your homework assignment when you bring it in tomorrow reminding me that you will run an errand for me. Thanks, Maria."

The following day, can you guess what happens? Maria anxiously turns in her assignment with a note, written in extra large print, reminding Mr. Harris that she will run an errand for him that day. Mr. Harris now implements the second part of his plan. He knows that the ball is back in his court and that his reaction to Maria right *now* could help to determine whether she begins to complete homework assignments. He looks at Maria, smiles, and says, "Thank you so much Maria, both for being responsible enough to complete your homework and for reminding me of something I would have very likely forgotten." He then sends Maria across the hall to deliver something very insignificant to the neighboring teacher.

What's Effective

 What Mr. Harris does with Maria is to simply think through his strategy and implement the simple principles of basic good psychology. Instead of engaging in a power struggle with Maria and daring her to forget her homework again "or else," he looks ahead and thinks about maintaining Maria's dignity, avoiding conflict, holding Maria accountable, and fostering a sense of responsibility in her so that she is more likely to complete future assignments. Brilliant? No. Good teaching? Yes.

Being teachers ourselves, we already know that some teachers may think, "That's not effective. He just rewarded her even though she turned in her assignment a day late. Besides, the only reason she completed the assignment was so that she would be able to run an errand. Teachers shouldn't have to reward students for living up to their responsibilities!" And that may be a typical reaction of another teacher, unless, of course, that teacher really thinks about what Mr. Harris has done. First of all, he did not tie the errand to the homework assignment as a reward, as he did not say that the only way she would be able to run the errand was if she turned in the assignment. He just used the assignment as a "way" for her to remind him of something he may forget. This was clever, in that had Maria forgotten the assignment again, reminding him verbally of the "errand" would have only called his attention to the fact that she had not completed the assignment. And when she did turn in the assignment, he chose his words carefully. He simply thanked her for being responsible. And by the way, thanking students for being responsible is one of the best ways of guaranteeing that they will continue to be responsible in the future. So Maria now feels like she has done something that has pleased her teacher, she does not have to deal with defending herself as to why she did not bring it in a day earlier, and the chances of her turning in future assignments increase greatly. Mr. Harris has definitely accomplished what he intended to accomplish. And he did it with no stress, without losing his temper, without engaging in a power struggle, and without daring the student, thereby making the student defensive. On second thought, maybe it was brilliant!

What's *Not* Effective

 What's not effective is the approach that some teachers continue to use. They become indignant over the fact that their students do not turn in homework assignments on time. In fact, they usually say things such as "Kids today! You can't get them to do anything *in* class much less *outside* of class." And, in their cases, they're usually right. These types of teachers, based upon their defeatist attitudes, usually cannot get students to accomplish much, either inside or outside of class. So they engage in desperate power struggles with their students, fostering an atmosphere of conflict and negative rapport. They assign too much homework, the work is not often seen by students as meaningful, engaging, or interesting, and they literally "dare" students not to complete the assignments with threats of doubling the homework, tripling it, etc. They also tend to give too much weight to homework assignments with regard to their students' final grades. Therefore, their success rates are low, their stress levels are high, and they tend to burn out quickly.

Although we are not trying to infer that homework is meaningless, we would like to share our beliefs that if teachers teach well, every single day, ensuring student success, then meaningful, interesting homework assignments, assigned in moderation, can enhance the overall learning experiences of students.

Bottom Line*

 Much research has been conducted and much controversy has arisen involving the "homework" question. Do students "need" homework? Does homework improve achievement? Does homework foster responsibility? Should homework affect student grades? The list goes on and on and so does the research. To date, the jury is still out on the homework issue.

Therefore, our suggestions to you are as follows:

♦ When you assign homework, do so in moderation.

♦ If you are one of several teachers who teach the same students, get together with those teachers and take turns assigning homework.

♦ When you do assign homework, make sure that the assignments are interesting, meaningful, and doable. Also, make sure that assignments provide for reinforcement in what has been taught—*not* new content. Students are much more likely to complete such assignments.

♦ Do not make a big deal out of missed homework assignments. (The old trick of doubling the amount, tripling the amount, etc. for students who do not turn in assignments has never worked. If they didn't do it once, they're not likely to do it twice.) However, if your school has a particular homework policy, follow the policy.

♦ Remember that all students do not go home to "ideal" households.

And most importantly, remember that you teach children—yes, even high school students are "children," and they need a break from their studies. For that matter, let's hope there's a little bit of a child left in all of us. If we could remember that, we'd all be a lot happier and a lot less stressed!

---

* The text for this section comes from Breaux, A.L. (2003). *101 "Answers" for new teachers and their mentors* (pp. 58–59). Larchmont, NY: Eye On Education. Used with permission.

> *I didn't know the answer, so I didn't raise my hand*
> *But the kid across the room who could answer on demand*
> *Had both hands in the air so high that I really couldn't see*
> *Why the teacher didn't call on him, but set her eyes on me.*
> *"Oh please," I begged in silent prayer, "don't let her call my name—*
> *For I am not as smart as he, and I will be ashamed."*
> *The teacher, much to my surprise, changed the question in mid-flight*
> *To one that she was certain I could surely answer right!*
> *So with enthusiasm, I answered really loudly*
> *And nowadays I must admit I'm feeling rather "proudly"!*
>
> Elizabeth Breaux

Getting Students to Participate

Classroom Scenario

During a recent fifth-grade math lesson, the teacher asked a question and several hands immediately went up. The student who was called on very enthusiastically blurted out a wrong answer—and we're talking about a blatantly wrong answer, far from even being close to any possible correct answer. Yes, it was the kind of answer that, if it were allowed, would generate giggles and jabs from other students. The teacher very calmly and pleasantly asked, "Would you mind explaining how you arrived at that answer?" The student began to explain—and the "reason" for the mistake became quite obvious to both the student and the teacher. In other words, in explaining how he had arrived at his answer, the student figured out his own mistake. At the moment of understanding, he said, "Aw man, I can't believe I did that."

The teacher first complimented him for finding his own error. Then she complimented him for making the mistake! She then asked the class, "Class, what do we know about mistakes?" The class, enthusiastically and in unison, broke into the following "jingle." On second thought, it was definitely more "rap" than "jingle." Regardless, here it is:

Mistakes are great—we just can't wait
Till someone makes another
Each time they do, they help us to
Learn more and discover
So let us take—this mistake
And learn a lesson from it
For when we do, we're able to
Get up each time we plummet!

The teacher then resumed her teaching without skipping a beat. Everything the teacher did with the students had an air of excitement about it. Her enthusiasm seemed to be contagious. The students were participating and, yes, they even seemed to be having lots of fun! The most amazing phenomenon of all was that the student who had made the mistake continued to volunteer his answers enthusiastically.

What's Effective

It is human nature to be afraid of being wrong! In general, students who do not understand the material, for whatever reason, are not likely to participate, any more than we as adults are comfortable participating in a conversation on a subject about which we are not familiar. So, we must help students to lose their *fear* of being wrong. We must instill in them our belief that *nothing* was ever learned without first making mistakes! This teacher obviously understood human nature and made it "okay" for her students to make lots of mistakes. She also made it "okay" for students to accept the mistakes of others and use them as learning opportunities for all.

Getting students to participate is a process that should begin with the students on the first day of school. First, put them at ease. To do this, ask them a simple question such as this: "What happened the first time you tried to feed yourself?" The answers will invariably be that a terrible mess was made. Then, discuss the possibility of having *never* been allowed to feed yourself! Have you ever seen adults who could not feed themselves? Make the point that it took many "tries" and much practice before we became efficient at that skill. Explain that it is the same for all skills. We *must* make mistakes in order to learn. Now, invite the students to "make lots of mistakes," because learning cannot take place without them! This is your opportunity as the teacher to put your students at ease. Let them know that you actually *welcome* the mistakes.

What's *Not* Effective

If you wanted to lose all possibility of students participating in your classroom, all you would have to do is to make sure that students are made to feel uncomfortable in making mistakes. We have all either committed, or witnessed some other teacher committing, one of the worst mistakes possible concerning encouraging participation—calling on the student whom we know is not paying attention in order to intentionally embarrass him in front of his peers! This is probably one of the best ways to "lose" a student for the rest of the year. The second greatest mistake we can make regarding student participation is to reprimand a student for making a mistake—a practice observed far too often in some classrooms. Embarrassing a student in front of his peers, for whatever reason, leads to anger, frustration, and possibly retaliation on the part of the student. If nothing else, it certainly serves to enable the student to "shut down" in the classroom. When students shut down, they don't participate. When students don't participate, they don't learn. Students who have shut down and have stopped participating usually begin participating in inciting discipline problems. It's a lose-lose situation.

Bottom Line

If you want to ensure active student participation, do the following:

   ◆ Plan lessons that involve the students as much as possible

   ◆ Be enthusiastic about whatever it is you are teaching

 ◆ Put students at ease, from day one, about participating

 ◆ Put students at ease, from day one, about making mistakes

 ◆ Let students see that everyone makes mistakes, and that mistakes are the ways in which we learn things

 ◆ Actually *encourage* mistakes and thus participation!

P.S. If you spot any mistakes in this book, please let us know. We'll be happy to participate in correcting them!

> *Raw, untamed, lacking*
> *Not by choice, but by the lack of wisdom gained through experience*
> *Shunned, ridiculed—not worth the time nor effort*
> *Our heads just above water, gasping for each breath*
> *Barely staying afloat, unable yet to swim*
> *We need you… why can't you see that?*
> *We'll never tell you, but we'll scream in peculiar ways*
> *Pretending not to care… do you really believe us?*
> *Please don't let us win—we need to lose so that you can win us over*
> *You are wiser—the leader for whom we hunger*
> *We can do it, but not alone*
> *We wear facades in order to survive. Don't you remember?*
> *We will follow a gentle hand, a loving heart, a knowing way, a kind word.*
> *We will conform to whatever is expected*
> *Please expect our best, or we will show you our worst*
> *We will act as we are treated, we will believe when we are believed*
> *We will trust when we are trusted, we will respect when we are respected*
> *Does it really matter who goes first?*
>
> Elizabeth Breaux

Handling "I Don't Care" Attitudes

Classroom Scenario

Says teacher A, "The students simply do not care! They accept zeroes as though they were candy! They refuse to turn in homework assignments. In fact, they won't even complete the in-class assignments. Several of them sleep in class on a daily basis. They are going to be in for a big surprise when report cards go out, and I'm not bending on those grades at all. Maybe all those F's will wake them up and alert them to how serious this really is!" (When report cards are finally issued, 48% of Teacher A's students receive failing grades.)

Teacher A's students also report to Teacher B. In teacher B's class, however, they are experiencing overwhelming success. Not a single student receives a failing grade on his report card. Just a few minutes observing in Teacher B's classroom reveals the reason.

What's Effective

 The same "failing" students are experiencing success in the classroom of Teacher B, so whatever Teacher B is doing is obviously working! Let's take a look and see what's happening in her classroom...

The students walk in after being greeted enthusiastically at the door, they take their seats, and the bell rings. Teacher B walks immediately to the front of the classroom where she sings a hearty "Good morning" and compliments them on their punctuality, telling them how fortunate she is to have them in her classroom.

All eyes are now on her. She conducts a short focus lesson on "Story Form," where she briefly recaps a story that was read yesterday, and students use individual sets of "manipulatives" (puzzle pieces) to find the conflict, climax, setting, characters, etc. The teacher guides them through this activity using an identical set of "manipulatives" on the overhead projector.

After guiding them through this and checking for understanding by encouraging student response and explanation, the teacher reads an interesting short story to them. She then hands out a new set of "manipulatives" and the students find the story parts on their own. The teacher walks around, monitoring, complimenting, and asking for explanations of wrong answers, which invariably lead to the correct answers! The teacher is simply oozing with enthusiasm. One would never believe that she has already taught this lesson twice today and has three classes remaining! The students don't know it either. It seems that each one truly believes that Teacher B is his/her teacher exclusively.

Responding to instruction, the students return the "manipulatives" to their individual bags, and one student collects them. Another student collects the desk charts and places them in the proper cubbyholes in the back of the room. Procedures are in place in this classroom and are practiced and implemented daily.

The following day, the teacher hands out a short quiz on "story form," and the students seem extremely eager to tackle it. These students are confident that they know the material and will receive a good grade. They are equally as anxious to have it graded. As the teacher picks up the short quiz (which took only thirteen minutes for all to complete), the students beg her to correct it immediately. Because of the nature of the quiz the teacher is able to correct it as one student hands out the individual class folders, which contain the "Grade Sheets."

Now for the really good part... All students remove their grade sheets from their folders and begin to write. These students record their own grades on their own sheets. The teacher, of course, keeps grades in her own roll book. The students do this each time they receive a grade...in anything! The enthusiasm with which they record their grades is undeniable. They have taken ownership of their grades in this class and are constantly aware of their averages.

The last student on each row then rises, collects the folders from the row, and places them in the correct cubbyhole. Instruction continues without skipping a beat. There is no doubt that this is the environment of a successful teacher with successful students.

(By the way, Teacher B is the one who, when asked by her administrator what would be a good day for an observation, replies, "Any time...just come on in.")

What's *Not* Effective

 Teacher A does not greet students at the door, nor does she do much to promote a positive classroom climate. She is, however, an accomplished "fault finder," and the students know it. Bell-work is not planned, nor is it implemented. Students are given a packet of worksheets, which they must complete at home if they do not finish in class. While students are working on today's packet of worksheets, the teacher sits at her desk grading yesterday's packet of worksheets. Because the work is meaningless to them, many have found alternate means of biding their time until the bell rings. One writes a letter to a friend while one shoots spitballs across the room. (A corner wall of petrified spitballs stands as evidence that he has become quite accomplished at this skill, considering all the days he has had to practice). One student is practicing a new and innovative technique for lacing basketball shoes while another is obviously completing some sort of arts and crafts assignment and has just hot-glued two Popsicle sticks to another student's back! The teacher, however, is oblivious to any of this because she is sitting at her desk intently grading papers! It goes without saying that those who do not value the assignment enough to do it in class will *certainly* not be spending time completing it at home.

Remember, now, that this is the teacher who said, "The students simply do not care! They accept zeroes as though they were candy! They refuse to turn in homework assignments; in fact, they won't even complete the in-class assignments. Several of them sleep in class on a daily basis. They are going to be in for a big surprise when report cards go out, and I'm not bending on those grades at all. Maybe all those F's will wake them up and alert them to how serious this really is!" *Please...*

Bottom Line

 First and foremost, please understand that "I don't care" usually means, "I don't understand, but I am not willing to admit that I don't understand." Therefore, "I don't care" attitudes are simply cover-ups for underlying problems. And, regrettably, sometimes the underlying problem stems from a lack of effective teaching. The fact is that "busy" work does not foster caring and achievement. However, it does foster "daring" and bereavement.

Do you want your students to "care?" Then teach effectively and with enthusiasm, relate all lessons to real life, make all tasks meaningful and doable, and your students will be successful. Success breeds success, caring breeds caring, and good teaching breeds student achievement!

THINGS TO CONSIDER: One of the things that makes teaching so difficult is the fact that we teach students, not textbooks and not grade levels. Each year, students come to us in all shapes, sizes, and colors, from all backgrounds, and yes, at all levels! Students are people, real people with unique abilities. And one of the things that makes the world "go round" is the fact that no two individuals are exactly alike. That's what makes teaching unlike any other profession! As teachers, we literally shape the future!

Teaching *All* Students at *All* Levels

Classroom Scenario

"I don't know how much longer I can do this," bemoaned Mrs. Turner. Every year, the students get farther and farther apart and farther and farther behind." "What do you mean?" asked a concerned colleague. "Well, I teach third grade, and I've got students on reading levels anywhere from first through fourth grades! My husband has students in 10th grade who are years behind level. We have this discussion every night. How can we prepare our students for the end-of-year criterion-referenced tests when many of them will just never get to where they need to be? It's just impossible to accomplish anything. If I teach to the middle of the class, which is what I have to do, then the lower students are "lost" and the higher students are "bored" to tears. That means discipline problems!

What's Effective

 It's too bad that Mrs. Turner has assumed this type of defeatist attitude. If she would only bother to look around her, she would see that her next door neighbor, Ms. Mitchell, also teaches third grade students—the same "levels" of students as Mrs. Turner— and she manages to succeed with all of them. Let's take a look inside of Ms. Mitchell's classroom and see the difference. (Remember, same grade level and same overall class make-up, meaning students of all shapes, sizes, backgrounds, achievement levels, etc. However, and most importantly, all of Ms. Mitchell's students are successful!) In speaking with Ms. Mitchell and watching her in action, we notice that first and foremost, her "attitude" and "philosophy" about teaching are quite different from Mrs. Turner's. This, in turn, makes for a totally different approach than that seen in Mrs. Turner's classroom. Ms. Mitchell says that she does not teach third grade, but rather she teaches students who happen to be in the third grade. She recognizes their varying levels of ability, achievement, maturation, experiences, backgrounds, etc. and so she accommodates all of those differences. But how? Is it even possible? Of course it is, but it's not easy. Ms. Mitchell, however, knows no other way. She teaches *students*, each and every one of them. When introducing a new skill, she plans exciting ways of getting the students motivated and interested. She then teaches and models the new skill for *all* of the students. Next, she guides them through the new skill by actually practicing with them. During this practice, it becomes obvious to Ms. Mitchell who understands, who requires a little more practice, and who requires remediation. She then sends those who are "ready" off on their own to practice the new skill independently. If she has a group of students who are "almost" there, she groups them and allows them to practice a little longer together. At the same time, she takes the ones who need some definite remediation and provides just that. Should it occur, and it does, that a student is capable of going above and beyond this particular skill, she has already planned for enrichment activities that will take that student to the next "level." And all of this is going on at the same time. It's all been planned. It happens with every lesson, because Ms. Mitchell knows that this will be the case with just about any skill she teaches, given the varying levels of students in any classroom.

When asked about her philosophy of teaching students at so many levels, she responds, "No two students are alike. And all students have particular strengths and weaknesses. Therefore, I take students from 'where they are' and I move them, methodically, step by step, to where they need to be. I don't waste my time complaining that they're so different. As a matter of fact, I'm grateful that they are, because it keeps the environment interesting and it keeps me on my toes. Anyone can be a 'successful' teacher with students who are already successful. But the 'real' teacher in me is put to the test with the students who are far behind their peers, who don't necessarily 'get it' right away, who need to utilize *my* strengths and talents in order to discover and develop their own.

Not surprisingly, Ms. Mitchell's students consistently enjoy some of the highest test scores in the district.

What's *Not* Effective

It goes without saying that the way Mrs. Turner and, obviously, Mr. Turner are teaching is *not* effective. And before they could possibly change their teaching methods, they would first have to change their "beliefs." They actually believe that it is impossible to teach students of varying levels in one classroom at the same time. Therefore, they do what many others who share this misconception continue to do—they teach "to the middle of the class." And by her own admission, Mrs. Turner comments that only the students who fall right in the middle, who are very few by the way, are actually able to benefit in any way. Imagine going to a doctor who says, "Sorry. But I simply cannot treat you because your symptoms are not 'average.' I only treat 'average' symptoms, and since you're really in need of special medical attention, there's simply nothing I can do for you. I'm only one person, and I cannot be expected to meet the needs of all patients." Sound ridiculous? Well, it's no more ridiculous than a teacher admitting that she does not even attempt to teach students who require the most attention.

Bottom Line

◆ The reality is that grade level does not normally equal achievement level. Students within one class setting will be performing at various levels of achievement. We must take them from where they are, not from where they are supposed to be or from where we would like for them to be.

◆ If you take a student who is performing below level and teach him "above" level, his chances of success are almost non-existent. However, if you take that same student and take him from where he is, teaching him at his level, the possibilities of achievement are limitless!

- The better the doctor, the better the patient's chances of recuperating from any given illness. The better the teacher, the better the student's achievement!

- With effective teaching, *nothing is impossible!*

> *I've never been too smart in school, and it's really very stressful*
> *But this year, I've got a teacher who makes sure I'm successful*
> *"All right! Way to go! Great job!" says my teacher*
> *Making me feel smart inside is truly her best feature!*
>
> Annette and Elizabeth Breaux

Ensuring Success for Every Student

Classroom Scenario

Mrs. Woe Is Me (Mrs. WIM) complained nonstop about a particular fourth-grade class. They were animals. They were the "low" group. Most had been retained at least once and had come to her unable to even write a complete sentence. They were reading and writing on a first to second-grade level, yet she was supposed to bring them up to grade level in time for the state assessment tests. "An impossible task," she insisted adamantly.

Remember the story "The Little Engine That Could?" ("I think I can, I think I can, I think I can...") Mrs. WIM obviously never read that one—too bad!

Well, despite the fact that they all *did* ultimately fail both Mrs. WIM's English/language arts class that year (surprise, surprise) and the language arts portion of the state test, the district insisted that they *were* teachable and reachable, considering the fact that they had passed, although barely, all of their other classes. Based on this fact, they were all promoted to 5th grade. "There you have it," said Mrs. WIM. "That's exactly what's wrong with education today. The students fail, and we pass them on."

"We pay, and you still don't teach," said the district coordinator to Mrs. WIM! (Just joking, but isn't that what we'd all love to say to the Mrs. WIMS?)

What's Effective

On to the 5th grade and to their new English teacher, Mrs. YESS (You're Each Successful and Special). As the students entered the room on one of those first days of school, they saw the following written in bold letters on the board: *"Because the dog ate the steaks. "* The students, of course, examined this carefully and then began to question its validity (which was exactly what Mrs. YESS wanted them to do). Mrs. YESS told them that this was the answer to a question. She then had the students volunteer possible "questions" that could have been answered with the response written on the board. (You know, the "Jeopardy" concept. Here's the answer. Now you supply the question.)

The students, of course, enjoyed this, soon realizing that there could be any number of questions resulting in the same answer—*"Because the dog ate the steaks."*

Next, Mrs. YESS had the students explain why this particular "answer" could be given in response to a variety of questions. After some probing, she managed to have all students tell her (notice that she did not tell them; she had them "tell her") that the answer, *"Because the dog ate the steaks,"* had not been written as a complete statement! Therefore, it was impossible to determine the exact question.

Mrs. YESS then quickly erased what was written on the board and replaced it with this complete sentence: *"We are having hot dogs tonight because the dog ate the steaks!"* She then presented them with the same scenario. "This is the answer to a question, "she said. "What is the question?" This time, of course, all students had the same response. The question is, agreed all students, "Why are we having hot dogs tonight?" She also managed to get the students to tell her, again, that the reason they could not all give the same "question" for the first "answer" was that the "answer" had been written as an incomplete sentence!

Mrs. YESS presented the students with several questions, and they answered using complete sentences: "What is your name?" "What is your favorite color?" and "Why are you here today?" She complimented them on their beautiful "complete sentences," and then quickly moved on to paragraph writing.

Mrs. YESS explained the "Five Finger Rule" of paragraph writing to the students, using her hand. "My thumb is my topic sentence," said Mrs. YESS. (She then discussed with the class the criteria used for writing a good topic sentence.) Mrs. YESS used a slide show to illustrate the topic sentence (written in blue). She used color-coding to help them see, understand, and remember. Mrs. YESS then explained that we should always use at least three details to support the topic sentence. Using her hand, she used her three middle fingers to represent three detail sentences. Three detail sentences then "appeared" on the screen, all written in red. "Finally," said Mrs. YESS, "we need a closing or 'wrap up' sentence. What do you do with a Christmas present before you place it under the tree?" asked Mrs. YESS. "Wrap it," said the students. "Exactly," replied Mrs. YESS. "We should also 'wrap' a paragraph before finishing it with a nice 'wrap up' sentence." A final sentence appeared on the screen, written in green.

With Mrs. YESS's guidance, the students then proceeded to write a paragraph of their own. They did it! A whole paragraph! Why? Because they finally understood the format.

Let's examine what just happened in ONE class period. The same students who could barely write a complete sentence, according to Mrs. WIM, were writing paragraphs after one lesson with Mrs. YESS! Amazing? Not really. What's amazing is that they had spent an entire year with Mrs. WIM, and, according to her, they still could not write a complete sentence.

After several days of writing and perfecting the format of paragraph writing, Mrs. YESS asked the truly "impossible" of her students. She would now have them begin essay writing! Imagine that! She began by explaining that an essay followed the same "Five Finger Rule" as the paragraph, only now they would be writing one topic paragraph, three detail paragraphs, and one closing paragraph!

Mrs. YESS handed an envelope to each student, and students were instructed to empty the contents onto their desks. The contents consisted of one blue paragraph (topic paragraph) cut into five individual sentences, three red paragraphs (detail paragraphs), cut into fifteen individual sentences (five per paragraph), and one green paragraph (closing or "wrap up" paragraph), cut into five individual sentences. She explained that what lay scattered in front of them was actually an essay, cut into separate sentences. With the constant assistance, encouragement, and enthusiasm of Mrs. YESS, the students pieced together the "puzzle" of their very first essay.

After this day, the students understood the format for writing a structured essay. They would begin working from here on the mechanics: sentence structure, spelling, transitions, grammar, etc., but now they had a good foundation on which to begin building. Some progressed more quickly than others, as will happen in every class, every day (if you teach more than one student), but Mrs. YESS remained mindful of moving each individual forward only when some level of success had been achieved. By the end of the year, not only did the students pass Mrs. YESS's language arts class, but they *all* passed the state's assessment! They had been "magically" transformed! By the way, many of them cried on the last day of school, along with Mrs. YESS…

What's *Not* Effective

 Let's examine what had caused these same students who had achieved such high levels of success in Mrs. YESS's class to have failed so miserably the previous year when "taught" by Mrs. Woe Is Me (WIM).

First, let's look at what Mrs. WIM had done:

- She had branded the students as "unreachable" from the first day of school.
- She had continued to have low expectations of them, based on their "histories."
- She had allowed them to continue to perform at low levels by refusing to challenge them.
- She had allowed them to continue to have low expectations of themselves through her refusal to challenge them.
- She had taught them using the old "lecture and assess" teaching technique that is ineffective, as we all know, for *any* student.
- She had "thrown" a lot of skill-work at them that was above their level, thereby setting them up for failure, day after day, week after week, month after month…a pattern to which they soon became accustomed, and which actually caused them to "regress" in their reading and writing skills!

Now, let's look at what Mrs. WIM had failed to do:

- She had failed to allow the students to achieve some success at their own levels (writing complete sentences, possibly, as Mrs. YESS had done) before trying to move them on.
- She had failed to be patient, attentive, concerned, caring, and enthusiastic.
- She had failed to create innovative, hands-on, activity-based lessons, which always help to motivate students.
- She had failed to become "real" to the students, probably because she had not enjoyed the challenge of teaching them.
- She had failed to motivate the students. As you remember from the scenario, she had actually deemed them the "animals" from the "low group." The words of a "teacher?"

Bottom Line

None of us ever learned anything at any level other than our own. It is only when we achieve and experience success at our own level that we can move forward. That does *not* mean that we ever allow students to stay "stuck" at one level. On the contrary, we help them to become successful at one level, then we immediately move them forward. That's why you will never find books entitled "Failure Breeds Success" or "How to Help Your Students Fail" or "The Joy of Failure" or "How to Solve Your Teaching Problems in the Lounge"!

Nothing inspires and motivates us more than our own successes. The fact is that we can *all* be successful at some level. Therefore, it is the job of the teacher to find that "level" for each student.

The absolute bottom line is this:

> No learning is ever wrought
> until the student is well taught.

THINGS TO THINK ABOUT: Would it be "fair" to use lots of visual aids when teaching a student who is visually impaired? Would it be fair to have all students attempt to run a mile? Can you run a mile? How "fair" would it be for a doctor to treat all 12-year-olds with the same medication, regardless of their unique illnesses? Treating students "fairly" does not mean treating them all the same. In fact, it means quite the opposite!

Treating Students Fairly

Classroom Scenario

It was the third week of school, his name was Eric, and he was often the last student to arrive to class. He always seemed to have some excuse as to why he was late, and it always involved the "fault" of someone else (naturally). The teacher never got upset and she did not make exceptions. She remained very consistent in implementing her rules, so Eric had been penalized several times for his tardiness. He and the teacher had talked about it, and he understood that she could not make exceptions for his being late to class, because it wouldn't be "fair" to the others in the class. Each time it happened, he would be penalized. Eric accepted this, but this still had not completely alleviated the problem. He was, however, becoming a little more punctual.

Unfortunately, Eric was involved in an accident where he broke a leg and sustained some other minor injuries. He did return to school shortly thereafter, confined to a wheelchair—the perfect excuse for tardiness, right?

Instead of allowing Eric extra time to get to class, the teacher decided to use a reverse approach (see Classroom Challenge 12). She called him in one day after the accident to let him know that she would do anything she could to help him through this difficult time. She informed him that she had already spoken to all of his teachers and made arrangements for each of them to dismiss him two minutes before the bell, thereby allowing him uninhibited passage through the hallways. Because of this, he would be able to arrive at his next class before everyone else and get himself situated with little interference from others. He thanked her for the help and seemed most appreciative.

Upon Eric's first "early" arrival to this class that day, the teacher thanked him in front of everyone for being so punctual in spite of the fact that he had a temporary handicap and complimented him on being such a "quick study" in maneuvering a wheelchair. She also pointed out to everyone how relentless Eric was becoming in his efforts to do his best in spite of his adversities. She made a specific effort to point out that a lesser person would have used his injury as an excuse not to do his best. (And by the way, once Eric had completely recovered from his injuries, he was never again tardy for class!)

What's Effective

 This teacher used a very effective technique—it's called being proactive. Instead of allowing the situation to even "begin" to get out of hand, she nipped it in the bud and beat Eric to the punch. (Sorry about the clichés, but they seem to make the point.) From day one, she had been fair and consistent, and Eric soon realized this. He was probably "testing" her to see if she really meant what she said. Obviously, she did. However, she never attacked Eric in any way. Rather, she enforced her rules and let him know why she did so. And slowly but surely, Eric was beginning to be a little more punctual.

When the unfortunate accident occurred, the teacher used basic good psychology and took some steps to see that the "wheelchair" need not become yet another of Eric's excuses. She did what was "fair" and allowed him some extra time, while at the same time she took steps to ensure that he would continue to be on time once the wheelchair was no longer necessary.

The simple fact is that we have never known a fair teacher to be ineffective or an unfair teacher to be effective. (That is, assuming that he or she possesses basic classroom management and teaching skills!) It all comes down to a matter of trust. When a child trusts you to handle any situation fairly, he or she will perform for you. It's that simple. This does not always mean that the child is "happy" with the outcome of a situation. But it does mean that the child understands and expects the outcome as a logical and fair consequence. The teacher in this scenario had been working quite diligently at earning the trust and respect of her students. She accomplished this with consistency and fairness.

Please understand that treating students fairly does not mean treating all students the same. If you have a student who is in a wheelchair, obvious exceptions to all rules might be applied. Common sense dictates this.

What's *Not* Effective

Because this teacher was human, just like the rest of us, she had become quite disgruntled with Eric's less than enthusiastic attitude. After all, he had been pushing the limit all year concerning prompt arrival to class. When seeing Eric in a wheelchair for the first time after the accident, a less effective teacher may have been tempted to forewarn him that using this as another "excuse" would not be tolerated. This approach, of course, would have been devastating in that it would have assured that the problem would remain ongoing.

Some teachers confuse "fairness" with "sameness." This is a mistake. It's as ludicrous as expecting doctors to treat all patients the "same" way, regardless of their individual medical needs. Treating patients "fairly" means doing what's best for them and their particular needs. Treating students "fairly" should be no different.

Bottom Line

Generally speaking, rules and procedures are written for and meant to be followed by everyone. This ensures effective management and instruction in the classroom setting. Remember, though, that treating students fairly does not always mean treating all students the same. It means treating each student in a manner that will evoke the best results from that particular student. Teachers who treat students fairly, implement procedures consistently, and enforce their classroom rules are admired, respected, and trusted by their students. Show us a teacher who treats students with consistency, dignity, and fairness, and we'll show you a successful teacher with a classroom of successful students. Fair enough?

Upside Down

You said that I could do it, but I didn't think I could
You seemed to know instinctively that "do my best" I would
But I sat there in defiance, my lip was hanging down
A snarled up nose and wrinkled brow; I uttered not a sound.
I wasted precious minutes, but you didn't seem to care
You said you had the time for me, when I'd need you you'd be there.
You didn't even notice all the paper that I tore
So finally I got busy and my thoughts I did explore.
And soon my mind was wandering to places far away
And I surprised myself with what my words began to say.
Once I'd finally finished and corrected all mistakes
I read it and I swelled with pride and thought, "My goodness sakes!
I am much better than the work I thought I would turn in
And I know you'll think I'm smart enough to do this well again!"
I think that I was smiling when I stood and turned around
When I realized you were watching me, my smile changed to a frown.
Then I watched you read my poem, and I saw you start to smile
And you put your arms around me, and you hugged me for a while.
And I tried my best to hide it, and to firmly hold my ground
But I couldn't stop that frown I wore from turning upside down!

Elizabeth Breaux

Getting Students "On Your Side"

Classroom Scenario

Every year, Ms. Chandler was assigned the "toughest" students in the high school—the ones no one else wanted. Her class was an "alternative" one, the school's self-designated halfway house. It consisted only of students who had previous histories of severe behavior problems. Most of her students had been expelled from school for a time. When they re-entered the school, Ms. Chandler's class was their first step. If a student could demonstrate improved behavior and an ability to succeed in a "normal" environment, he would move on to "normal" classes. Interestingly, but not surprisingly, Ms. Chandler's classroom was a revolving door. It never failed. She had done this for the past ten years and not once had a student failed to earn the "privilege" of exiting her class and returning to the mainstream. It was also interesting, but not surprising, to note that many of the students, after returning to the mainstream, would eventually be sent back to Ms. Chandler. Again, it never failed. A student would experience a complete "transformation" with Ms. Chandler and thus exit the class. The same student would then experience a complete "reversal of fortune" and be sent back to Ms. Chandler's class. Once again, transforming and exiting. Once again, reverting and entering. The "normal" teachers blamed the inevitable "reversal of fortune" on the fact that these students simply could not survive in the mainstream. Yes, they might be successful in Ms. Chandler's "abnormal" environment, but as soon as they were placed in "normal" classrooms, they would revert to their delinquent ways.

A closer analysis of the situation, involving classroom observations in both the "normal" and "abnormal" classrooms, interviews with the "delinquents," and interviews with the teachers, was quite revealing. The "mystery" was solved, once and for all! The case of the "abnormal" students will now unfold, point by point.

What's Effective

- ◆ Ms. Chandler treated the "abnormal" students as "normal" students.
- ◆ Ms. Chandler was always upbeat and enthusiastic.
- ◆ Ms. Chandler welcomed every student to her classroom.
- ◆ Ms. Chandler made each student feel worthy, appreciated, and special.
- ◆ Ms. Chandler *loved* her students. She would actually shed tears, both tears of joy and selfish tears of sorrow, when a student moved on to a more "normal" environment.
- ◆ Ms. Chandler found a way to make every student successful.
- ◆ Ms. Chandler was patient. She never engaged in power struggles with students.
- ◆ Ms. Chandler's students actually admitted that they loved her class so much that they were willing to do whatever it took to get

placed back in her room. And, of course, severe misbehavior was "what it took."

What's *Not* Effective

- The "normal" teachers treated Ms. Chandler's students as "abnormal."
- The "normal" teachers demonstrated a lack of enthusiasm in their teaching.
- The "normal" teachers made Ms. Chandler's students feel "different" and "abnormal."
- The "normal" teachers admitted "no love loss" when a student was sent back to Ms. Chandler's classroom.
- The "normal" teachers would not ever be accused of "bending over backwards" to make Ms. Chandler's students successful.
- The "normal" teachers exhibited extreme impatience with Ms. Chandler's students. They frequently engaged in power struggles with the students in their classrooms—both the "normal" and "abnormal" students.
- The "normal" teachers cried "tears of *joy*" upon sending a student back to Ms. Chandler.

Bottom Line

When you take a child, any child, and do whatever it takes to make him feel appreciated, worthy, special, and successful, he will respond in a "normal" way. What's a "normal" way? A "normal" way, for any child (or adult), is to act toward others as he is treated by others. There's no rocket science involved here! You get a student on your side by being on his side. Therefore, even abnormal students will act normally when treated normally. And even normal students will act abnormally when treated abnormally. Thus, normal teachers who act abnormally will experience normal responses from their students, which, in this case, would mean "abnormal" behavior.

Do you want your students on
your side? Be on theirs!

You just said to "do" it, but I didn't do it well
My goal was just to finish; I cared not to excel
You didn't seem to notice that my work was nothing grand
I could have done much better; (I don't think you understand)
You see I'm just a little kid, and not yet can I see
The importance of this task at hand to the person I will be
So if you want to see the very best that I can do
Then you will have to reach inside, grab on and pull me through
I'm warning you, I'll kick and scream, pretending not to care
And rest assured I'll never show what's hidden deep in there
So please don't take it personally when I act in wicked ways
Just clench your teeth and smile and find the best in me to praise.

Elizabeth Breaux

Recognizing Student Strengths

Classroom Scenario

It was the third week of school and a new student was assigned to Mrs. Bartlett's 3rd grade class. His name was Juan. Juan, of course, came with a history—a history of low achievement, of defiance, of a troubled family life, and of several attempts made by three prior schools to "classify" him as one in need of special education services. However, none of these attempts thus far had been "successful." His reading level was that of a first-grader. His math skills were those of a second-grader. And his social skills—well, let's just say that Juan had lots of room for growth. The principal, on learning of Juan's history, had intentionally assigned Juan to Mrs. Bartlett's class. Why? Because Mrs. Bartlett was a true artist in her teaching. She had the rare quality of finding the good in all students and nurturing their strengths as opposed to dealing with their faults. She had been teaching for almost three decades and often enjoyed letters and visits from former students who claimed they owed much of their successes in life to her influence. But could she work her magic with Juan? Read on.

What's Effective

Mrs. Bartlett immediately established a personal relationship with Juan and welcomed him to the class. (Believe it or not, it was the first time that Juan had ever been officially "welcomed" to a classroom.) She spent extra time on those first few days getting to know him, telling him about herself, and finding out what really interested Juan. She soon learned that Juan had a fascination with color and with art. On one wall of the classroom, there was a "brag board" where all students were featured. They brought in pictures of themselves, wrote about their accomplishments, posted their dreams, and proudly displayed anything and everything that told a story of who they were as individuals. On the very first day, Mrs. Bartlett asked Juan to bring a picture or two of himself. Juan said he had none. Mrs. Bartlett immediately pulled out her instant camera and took Juan's picture. She put it up on the "brag board" that very day. Though it soon became obvious that Juan struggled with academics, Mrs. Bartlett did not let that discourage her from her mission—that of making Juan successful. She did not attempt to force the "3rd grade curriculum" down Juan's throat. Instead, she began teaching him at his own level where she knew he would immediately experience success. And he did! She complimented him daily on his accomplishments and told him that she recognized an amazing amount of potential in him. She proudly displayed every piece of artwork Juan could bring to her. The more she displayed, the more he brought in for her approval. She used her "teacher creativity" to relate almost everything she taught him to the world of art, of color, of shape, of form, of beauty. In teaching him to write, she had him write about art. In teaching him to read, she had him read about art. She did this with everything she taught him. Soon, Juan began to excel—not just in his artistic endeavors but in his academic endeavors. By the end of the year, he showed more academic growth than any other student in the class and duly received an award. Today, many years later, he is a successful career artist (possessing a college degree) designing advertisements for commercial businesses. He makes more money than any classroom teacher and supports a wife and two beautiful children. He still visits Mrs. Bartlett.

What's *Not* Effective

The "Juans" of the world are in every classroom. Regrettably, however, many "Juans" never experience the success that they could. Some are lost in the shuffle. Some are ignored by those who teach them. Many never have the opportunity to be taught by a Mrs. Bartlett. Remember, Juan had a "history" of low achievement and defiance. In some classrooms he would have continued on that path. Had Mrs. Bartlett failed to "dig deep" and uncover the strengths and talents that Juan possessed, he would have most certainly fallen farther behind and become more defiant. The course of his future would have been negatively impacted. He would have very likely been retained and eventually could have become a real discipline problem. As many overage students, he would have very likely dropped out of school and "hit the streets" far too young and far too inexperienced. Without an education, he could have become yet another statistic!

The Bottom Line

 In the words of Oscar Wilde, "No great artist ever sees things as they really are. If he did, he would cease to be an artist." We take the liberty of paraphrasing Mr. Wilde's quote to fit the context of teaching… "No great teacher ever sees students as they really are. If he did, he would cease to be a teacher." As teachers, it is our privilege to take raw materials that we are given, our students, and discover the talents and strengths that are unique to each. In discovering those strengths, we uncover them. When they are exposed, we can help to develop them. True greatness, true strength, and true talent lie within each student. As sculptors of students, we take the ordinary and chip away to the extraordinary. We reveal what lies beneath and in doing so, we change the world, one child at a time.

> *Give me an ounce of inspiration*
> *Leading, of course, to motivation,*
> *Which will spark my imagination*
> *Thus, you'll see my perspiration*
> *As I feel my mind's vibration*
> *Spurring on my new creation*
> *Concentration for the duration*
> *Whew! I did it! Pure elation!*
>
> Annette L. Breaux

Motivating Students

Classroom Scenario

Mrs. Inspiration (Okay, so it's not her real name, but it should be!) greeted her 8th grade students at the door as always, shaking their hands and patting them on the back as well, while giving a hearty "how are you today" or "glad you're back, we missed you yesterday" to each student who entered her room.

On this day she began the class by writing the word "supernatural" on the board. A class discussion immediately ensued on the meaning of the word. Several of the students injected examples of the "supernatural" from movies that they had seen or books they had read. She then had them discuss their individual feelings concerning the topic. After the discussion she admitted to the class that she had never believed in supernatural occurrences, but a recent experience in her life had given her cause to reexamine her outlook. All eyes were upon her as she began her story and an observer could have "heard a pin drop" in the room. Here is her story:

"I grew up very close to my grandfather, Pop," explained Mrs. Inspiration. "I spent a lot of time with him, both in my childhood and adult years. Actually, I had even spent nights at his house on many occasions since becoming a teacher."

"As you all know, I am an 'early bird' who likes to arrive at school early in the morning. Whenever I would sleep at my grandparents' house, I was always terrified that the old alarm clock, the one next to the bed in the room where I slept, would not work. Pop, however, would always set his own alarm clock and come to awaken me at 5:00 a.m., my usual awakening time."

"This went on for many years until, unfortunately, Pop passed away during school holidays a couple of years ago. I stayed with my grandmother, Mom, through the holidays. I will never forget how worried I was when getting into bed on the night before school started again. I did set that old alarm clock, but I went to sleep worried that it might not work, knowing that Pop was no longer there to make certain that I awakened on time."

"I was sleeping quite soundly when a huge crash in the room startled me from my sleep. I jumped up and out of bed, thinking first that a car had crashed through the room (judging from the intensity of the sound). Immediately upon looking around, I observed that Mom's box of art supplies, which she kept neatly stacked in a corner of the room, had been scattered throughout the room! The supplies were literally *everywhere*! At that very moment, the clock caught my eye—it was 4:59 a.m.! I instantly knew, in my heart, what had just happened. It was not frightening to me, but rather it was very comforting. I am sure that Pop just wanted to make certain that I was awake (in case that old alarm clock would not have worked)."

"You see, students," said Mrs. Inspiration, "people could rationalize this incident in any number of ways, but I choose to believe that Pop was just hanging around to take care of me one last time."

It goes without saying that every student in that classroom was totally enthralled with the story, and what Mrs. Inspiration did next to "break the silence" was unforgettable. She said to them, "Okay, students, now that I have shared my story with you, I want for you to consider what it may feel like to be placed in a similar situation. The story that we are about to read is about a young man who has a very similar experience. As you read, I ask you to stop occasionally, closing your eyes, and imagining that you are the young man in the story."

What happened next was amazing. It was as though a magic fairy had waved her wand over all of the students and made them instant lovers of the written word! They were all reading, smiling, closing their eyes (as Mrs. Inspiration had suggested that they do) and flipping through the pages with eager anticipation of what lay ahead. The ensuing discussion was enlightening, exciting, inspirational, and inviting. Everyone shared, everyone questioned, everyone wondered. Suddenly the bell rang and they all reported to Mrs. Exasperation's class.... (You guessed it. We'll read about her under "What's *Not* Effective.")

What's Effective

Mrs. Inspiration knew that she had to find a way to motivate students so that they would "want" to read the selected story. She put much thought and effort into this. She knew, as do all effective teachers, that by inspiring them with a real-life story, she could get them interested and eager to read. She also used a clever way of having them place themselves in the position of the story character. And *it worked*! Mrs. Inspiration became "real" to the students by sharing a real-life experience of her own. Just that simple act of sharing, to students, is motivating and inspiring. Mrs. Inspiration motivated her students by inspiring them with a real-life experience that actually inspired her to be more motivational in her teaching! Wow!

Because she was a reading teacher, she knew that people in general (adults included) are not motivated to read unless there is a "reason." So why is it that in the typical reading class, students are often expected to just "want" to read a selection that was chosen by someone else for them? (Read on…if you are "motivated" to do so.)

What's *Not* Effective

Okay…on to Mrs. Exasperation. You all know her, because she was your worst nightmare when you were in school. Remember the students in Mrs. Inspiration's class? The attentive, eager, motivated "book gobblers?" Well, here they are again, only something "supernatural" has obviously happened to them somewhere in the transition between classes.

They entered their American History class. What could be more real and motivating than the history of our own ancestors, right? *Wrong*!

"Open your textbooks to page 78," instructed Mrs. Exasperation (in a less than jovial tone). "Today you are going to read about the Civil War. Please read pages 78–94 and answer the questions at the end of the chapter. And I want to see everyone working. You may begin. Anything that you are unable to complete in class will become homework."

Is there any reason to expound on why Mrs. Exasperation's teaching "technique" was not effective? We didn't think so.

Bottom Line

 In a perfect world all students would enter our classrooms motivated, enthusiastic, and eager to learn. Not only is that idealistic and unrealistic, but it is also boring. Where does the challenge lie? Would we even be needed? The fact is that if we, as teachers, are waiting for the students to come to us already motivated, then we are waiting on a ship that has been lost at sea! Actually, it was never set afloat. It was never even built!

Remember that we cannot "teach" our students until we "reach" our students. Motivating students is part of the "reaching" phase, which is a prerequisite for the teaching/learning phase. In other words, if there had been a ship and you decided to cast your line into the ocean, you would have had to "hook" the fish before you could reel it in! No fish will be "caught" until they are hooked. No students will be "taught" until they are hooked!

Our hope is that this book will serve as a hook, a motivator (on those days when you are somewhat less than motivated), providing you with the motivation to be so obviously motivated that your students will scurry to jump onto the motivational ship along with you!

FACT: When "substitute" teachers enter classrooms, the students often "substitute" their own personalities with ones that are much less desirable!

Providing for Substitute Teachers

Classroom Scenario[*]

I remember it like yesterday. It was my first year of teaching and I had to attend a meeting. It was going to be the first day of school that I had ever missed. Still wearing my rose-colored glasses and never having left my seventh graders in the hands of a substitute teacher, I never anticipated what "could" and probably "would" happen during my absence. I thought I had all of my bases covered. I had left explicit instructions for the substitute teacher—down to the last detail. I told my students I would be out, that a substitute teacher would be with them, and that I would see them the day after. By this time I had my classroom management system well organized. My students knew what I expected, and they followed all of my procedures beautifully. So I had nothing to worry about. Right? Oh, how very wrong! I returned the following day to learn that my little "angels" had turned into raging devils in the hands of the substitute. The substitute vowed never to come near my class again. She was devastated and so was I. How could this have happened? What had gone wrong? I learned the hard way that I had missed one crucial step. Yes, I had provided the substitute teacher with explicit instructions, but I had totally forgotten about the instructions for my students. So just as the poor, unsuspecting substitute teacher vowed never to enter my classroom doors again, I vowed never to let such a situation occur again should I be absent.

---

[*] The text for this section comes from Breaux, A.L. (2003). *101 "Answers" for new teachers and their mentors* (p. 41). Larchmont, NY: Eye On Education. Used with permission.

What's Effective[**]

The solution was quite simple and worked like a charm! The next time I had a meeting to attend, this is what I did, step by step:

- ◆ I told my students I would be absent and that I would need for them to take over the classroom and help the substitute teacher. I made a big deal over that fact that I knew I could trust them, so I was confident that things would run smoothly.

- ◆ I assigned roles to each student. For instance, one student had the task of welcoming the substitute and showing her where everything was located on my desk. Another student had the job of handing out the bellwork assignment to classmates as they entered the classroom. Another student had the job of giving the signal for quiet when the substitute was ready to begin and sharing that same signal with the substitute so that she could use it also. Another student had the job of explaining all of the daily procedures to the substitute. Another had the job of picking up assignments from students as they finished their work. I kept making up "jobs" until every student had one. One student even had the job of presenting the substitute with a small gift to show their appreciation at the end of the class period. Another had the job of "beginning the applause" after the gift was given. All students shared the job of thanking the substitute on the way out of the classroom, and one student was assigned to remind any student who forgot. Okay, you get the picture.

- ◆ On the day before I was to be absent, we practiced by pretending that I was the substitute. The students loved the idea, because now they were in charge of running the classroom and helping to make things easy on the substitute teacher. They had specific responsibilities, and they took pride in that fact.

- ◆ I wrote down all responsibilities of every student and each got a copy. This would help to ensure that they would hold each other accountable or simply remind each other if one of them forgot their assigned job.

- ◆ We also discussed the fact that this same plan would remain in place if I were ever absent due to illness. For this, we kept an extra "gift" in the closet.

[**] The text for this section comes from Breaux, A.L. (2003). *101 "Answers" for new teachers and their mentors* (pp. 41–42). Larchmont, NY: Eye On Education. Used with permission.

Results? I returned the day after my absence to find a two-page letter from the substitute. She said to *please* call her if I ever needed a substitute again. She went on to say that she had never witnessed anything like it. She was amazed at how helpful and cooperative the students were. "And can you believe that they actually clapped for me at the end of the class? I've never received applause in my life! And I believe that every single one of them stopped to thank me on the way out." You see, the students had played their roles so well that she didn't even realize that most of it had been rehearsed and that they were "supposed" to stop and thank her on the way out.

The students couldn't wait to brag about how well they had run the class without me! It worked for me every time I used it over the years, it worked for every teacher I shared it with, and it will work for you!

What's *Not* Effective

What's *not* effective is *not* having a plan for substitutes. And even if you do have a specific plan for substitutes, you must prepare your students beforehand and have a plan for them! Don't make the mistake of many teachers by "expecting" that your "angels" will remain angels in the event of your absence. Chances are that they won't. That is, unless you have planned well and practiced with them *before* the chance to be devils arises. *Not* having a plan for both the substitute teacher and the students will result in an unpleasant journey to the fiery depths of *chaos*!

Bottom Line

♦ Students often "substitute" their personalities for less desirable ones in the presence of a substitute teacher.

♦ Actual learning can and does take place in the hands of a substitute teacher if the students are well-prepared and well-rehearsed and specific plans have been left for the substitute teacher.

♦ Students will rise to meet your expectations of them. Set your expectations beforehand and then give your students the responsibility of making the substitute teacher's experience a pleasant one.

♦ The fact is that you *will* be absent, for various reasons, from time to time. If you want to ensure that your "angels" will remain "angels," then teach them how *not* to be devils in the hands of a substitute. Prepare them well, have a plan for the substitute, and leave your heavenly environment knowing that all is well cared for on the wings of angels!

Dealing
with Yourself

If I could just deal with everyone else and not have to deal with me
Life would be good, as I know I could be a wonderful "Dear Abby"
But having to deal with myself isn't easy—it's actually very hard
For dealing with only my "stuff," I guess, I would never receive an award
It's easy to give advice, you see—and actually I'm quite good
But I don't always take my own advice, though I know that I really should
So I'm starting to look in the mirror today, and I'll deal with the one
*   looking back*
And I'll stop trying to find fault with everyone else, to make up for
*   whatever I lack...*

Annette L. Breaux

> *I had a plan to make a plan,*
> *My New Year's resolution,*
> *But since I failed to plan the plan*
> *This still was no solution.*
> *The plan did not materialize*
> *I did not follow through*
> *First you have to plan the plan*
> *Then do what you plan to do!*
>
> Annette and Elizabeth Breaux

Planning Effectively

Classroom Scenario

Every year all social studies students in the school are given the assignment of turning in projects for the social studies fair. Every year Teacher A not only has several winners but has more participants than any other teacher in the school. She invariably has students who place at the regional and the state levels. Coincidence, or just a well-planned format for success?

Teacher A hands out the packet with instructions for social studies projects. The packet itself, which is distributed to all students in the district, gives all guidelines along with the due date. Teacher A uses this to construct her own rubric/checklist of "mini due dates" for different components of the project. Points are not only awarded for turning in parts on time, but extra points are awarded for early submittal of components. Because the teacher realizes the importance of modeling, she shares with the students the video tape of last year's students along with their projects. During the video students explain their projects along with the process that led them to be successful. Not only does watching this video give students a focal point, but seeing last year's students' successes is a huge motivator. The teacher also holds one-on-one talks with her students to discuss progress on the projects. The teacher gives advice and guides students but does not *do* the projects for them. As individual components are turned in, the teacher fills in that portion of the rubric so that students can watch their gradual accumulation of points. (Points are deducted for components turned in late. Parents are notified if students are late, so as to keep them up-to-date on progress.)

What's Effective

 Because the projects are viewed as a process that can ultimately end in success, as opposed to simply another assignment, and because of the huge amount of support that they are given by their teacher, it is no wonder that the better projects have traditionally come from this teacher's classes.

Does this method take some extra work, commitment, and dedication on the part of Teacher A? Absolutely! Is it worth it? Just ask Teacher A. (You already know her answer.) We've all heard the old saying, "If you fail to plan, you are planning to fail." This is especially true in the classroom. Effective instruction is reliant on proper planning. There is no way around it. Anyone who tells you that this is easy has *never* been a teacher. It's hard work, but effective classroom teachers know that bypassing the planning stage is a sure prescription for failure.

Imagine leaving to go on vacation with your family without having planned the trip! You are all in the car, but you have not properly packed, you have no destination in mind, no roadmap, no money, and no gas in the car! What are the chances that this trip will be a successful one? Okay, so maybe you get really lucky and things work out for the best. The point here is that the chances of this being a successful trip would be much greater if the trip were properly planned. Having a little money wouldn't hurt either, unless you plan on finding part-time work along the way....

The same holds true in the classroom. We are *never* as effective if we "wing it" as we are when we plan it. It's that simple. Planning is one of the most difficult parts of teaching. It takes time, patience, an understanding of effective teaching, an understanding of each year's students' and classes' specific needs, and loads of creativity. Any effective teacher will tell you that the hard work is in the planning. If you plan an effective lesson, then you can really have "fun" when it comes to teaching it. If you don't plan an effective lesson, then you are going to be on pins and needles while teaching, trying to think of what to do next, appearing disorganized to the students, and inviting chaos. Both you and the students will definitely suffer.

What's *Not* Effective

 To illustrate what's *not* effective, let's look into the classroom of Teacher B. We all know Teacher B, because we have either been taught by her, taught next door to her, or have had children of our own suffer through her class. Teacher B receives the same packet of information as did Teacher A, only teacher B's students receive it one week later. (It is not priority for Teacher B because she already knows that her students are doomed for failure on the projects. Is it any wonder?)

Teacher B hands out the packets, instructs the students to read over them carefully, informs them that it is *"for a grade,"* and then leaves it entirely in their hands. She will probably remind them the week before the due date, and will certainly show her disappointment in their lazy attitudes and sloppy work ethics when the projects are either not turned in or are turned in poorly completed.

Remember, however, that Teacher B always has an excuse for why Teacher A's students perform so well in comparison to her students. "Teacher A just gets the good kids every year!"

Bottom Line

 Effective teachers are effective planners. Effective teachers know that *not* planning is a sure way to ensure that students will *not* be successful. There is no room for procrastinators in the teaching profession. Have you planned tomorrow's lessons yet? If not, put this book down and get busy planning!

FACTS: The key to time management is "management." If you don't manage your time, it will begin to manage you! Also, if you really want to get technical about "time," read Einstein's theory. If you don't have "time" to read it because you're too busy teaching, read the challenge below. We think we can help!

Managing Your Time Wisely

Classroom Scenario

The tardy bell rings and Teacher A doesn't even notice. Nor do the students. Some are in the classroom but few are in their seats. Some are still loitering in the hallway. Some are skipping class. (The rest are peaking into the window of Teacher B's class—*big mistake*!) While Teacher A is screaming down the hallway for those not within an ear's reach, a scuffle has begun in the classroom. While the teacher is putting out the "fire" in the classroom, those in the hallway are inching ever so slowly toward the room. After all, there is no consequence for being late. As Teacher A returns to the hallway to scream for a second time, Johnny throws a book at Travis who has just accused him of stealing a pencil from his desk.

For bellwork, students are given an abundance of notes to copy from the overhead projector, a meaningless task, which they view as such. Several insist that they cannot see the overhead projector; a few have lost their notebooks; Travis no longer has a pencil and is suffering a concussion after being hit in the head with a book!

Obviously, the clock is ticking and precious time is being wasted. And this is only the beginning of class! We won't go on to describe what the rest of this chaotic class period entails, as we're sure you can imagine that one for yourself. But we will add that this is the class that always leaves several minutes *early* for lunch! Where's the instruction?

Now on to Teacher B, thank goodness! The tardy bell rings and Teacher B's door closes. All students are in class and bellwork begins immediately.

The bellwork assignment has been carefully planned with attention paid to getting students excited about today's lesson. A tardy chart with each student's number (never use names) can be observed on the wall. "Xs" have been placed next to numbers to show total numbers of "tardies" to date. (Very few "Xs" exist on the chart, however.) Students know that after three "Xs" they will be sent to the office where one of several consequences will be administered. This is school/district policy. Because the teacher follows the policy from day one, students know what to expect and are seldom, if ever, late for Teacher B's class. Teacher B is never seen screaming in the hallway. Instead, Teacher B simply makes students aware of the policies and procedures and follows them consistently.

Teacher B uses supply boxes (boxes that each student has supplied and that remain in the classroom), so no time is wasted trying to provide students with pens, pencils, etc. Bellwork, which relates to the lesson of the day, is interesting, stimulating, and thought provoking. One activity flows seamlessly into the next. Teacher modeling followed by active student engagement is the rule in this class. The students are learning by seeing and doing. Wow!

This is the classroom where the dismissal bell sometimes catches everyone off-guard, because they are too busy actively learning to be watching the clock. It's the classroom where students are often heard saying, "Is that the bell already?"

The bell rings to signal the end of the instructional period and students scurry out of the classrooms. Some wait around for friends, some play around in their lockers, some get into trouble, while others are hurrying to get to their next class on time. Why this difference in attitude and behavior? Obviously, some are going to the classrooms of the Teacher A's of the school, and the others are going to the classrooms of the Teacher B's.

What's Effective

 Those students hurrying to get to their next classes on time are going to the same handful of teachers in the school—the teacher B's. They are going to the classrooms where it is of utmost importance to be on time in order to avoid missing anything! These teachers have a tardy policy and they follow it! They also structure every single minute of instructional time. Imagine that!

Bellwork is not wasted/busy time. It can take many shapes and forms, but is always meaningful and is an introduction to today's lesson. Students know that what they do for the first few minutes will be useful during the remainder of the class. Since they see it as important, they *do it*!

What's *Not* Effective

 What's not effective is *not* having a plan, not implementing rules and procedures, and not managing every second of precious instructional time. Period!

Bottom Line

 Unless the teacher has effectively implemented procedures and effectively planned for instruction, time management is not even possible! There is no doubt about it—a classroom where procedures are properly practiced and implemented will run like a well-oiled machine, thereby making time management not only effective, but easy! It makes perfect sense. If students are expected to be on time, and they know what is expected of them from the moment they walk into your classroom, effective instruction can begin immediately without wasting time!

So why isn't everyone doing it?

Refraining from Complaining

Refraining from complaining doesn't stop the sky from raining
What it does do, however, which is really really clever,
Is it does change the weather—the weather of your mood
And you can weather any storm—just change your attitude!

Annette L. Breaux

Adjusting Your Attitude

Classroom Scenario

It was going to be another long, trying day. The absentee list had just been delivered and Joseph Jones was not listed. "If he so much as opens his mouth to breathe today, I will scream!" thought Mrs. Wilson, trying to mentally prepare for his arrival (which came sooner this day than expected).

As fate would have it, Joseph's first period teacher was absent, and Joseph had been assigned to Mrs. Wilson for first period today, in addition to his regularly scheduled second period class! "That's it," thought Mrs. Wilson. "I cannot possibly survive this! Either he will be gone by the end of the period, or I will be gone...."

"Pull this desk into the corner and have a seat, young man," she demanded as Joseph entered the room. "Put your feet in front of your desk facing the wall and do not turn around, or you are going straight to the office! I have thirty students in here who want to learn, and I will not allow you to disrupt them!"

Joseph, of course, having to "save face" in front of his peers, reacted in a typical fashion. He snatched the desk from Mrs. Wilson, dragged it directly over several students' feet, intentionally trying to initiate a confrontation, and then slammed it into the corner of the room. He then threw his books onto the floor, dropping heavily into his seat and kicking the wall as he turned to "face it," as he had been directed to do. Note that until now he had followed the teacher's directives precisely. All she had directed him to do was to pull the desk into the corner and sit facing it. She did not specify the "manner" in which this was to be done, and he knew that. He was a master at "walking that line."

The remainder of the class period was just as Mrs. Wilson had expected, and by the way, precisely as she had "set it up" to unfold. She spent the rest of the period reprimanding Joseph, as he continued to make noises, get out of his seat, gesture to others, etc.

What's Effective

 Imagine, if you can, that instead of having "set Joseph up" for failure, Mrs. Wilson had decided to "set him up for success." That's a hard one, as Mrs. Wilson knew Joseph and already "expected" the worst from him. (See Teaching Challenge 8, "Please expect our best, or we will show you our worst.")

Expecting the best from Joseph would have required "the best" from Mrs. Wilson. And often times, our "best" requires a major adjustment of *our* attitudes. Her best would have looked something like this:

"Good morning Joseph! How are you today? I'm so lucky to have you in two classes today. Since this is not your regularly scheduled class, I was wondering if I could get you to help me with a few things. You have really been acting so much more responsibly lately, and I'd like for you to staple and file some papers for me. First, let me show you where everything is located, as I will be teaching the class and you will be on your own. If you need anything, just quietly raise your hand, and I will get to you as soon as I can. Thank you so much, Joseph. I am so fortunate to have such a helpful, responsible young man here to assist me. I'll make sure to phone your mother and let her know what a huge help you were to me today."

Wow! Can you imagine any child, regardless of previous behaviors, not responding positively to such treatment? Mrs. Wilson could have "opened the door" to having Joseph "eating out of the palm of her hand," "wrapped around her little finger," and "walking through fire" for her, instead of his having her "in hot water," "fit to be tied," and "ready to blow!" (This officially "wraps up" our lesson on Figures of Speech....)

What's *Not* Effective

 Obviously, both Mrs. Wilson's attitude and approach were *not* effective. Not only did she end up having to deal with Joseph's "bad" behavior, but she had actually encouraged it! She "set him up" for failure. She "expected his worst" and he gave it to her. She did not call on those innate acting abilities that all teachers must possess. Remember, kids don't know whether or not we are acting. They simply respond to our attitudes and behaviors in the manner delivered to them.

Bottom Line

 Students' attitudes will mirror yours. We must constantly be examples of the attitudes and behaviors that we want "mirrored" back to us. As has often been said, we may not be able to be in control of all of the circumstances around us, but we can *always* be in control of our attitudes! Teachers are the best actors and actresses in the world! We earn academy awards on a daily basis! The better our attitudes, the better the attitudes of our students! The better the attitudes of our students, the easier it is for us to maintain a positive attitude. The more negative a student's attitude, the more positive we have to be. Remember, we are professionals, and our attitudes, whether real or feigned, must be attitudes of professionals, *at all times*, especially when times are difficult.

"And the Oscar goes to…"

Controlling Your Actions and Reactions

Classroom Scenario

There were 60 students in the seventh grade at this particular school. The two classes were divided equally and taught by two teachers. At recess the final plans were made and the grand scheme would finally materialize. The plans had been well laid and the students were ready. Today, the teachers had an early morning faculty meeting. This always meant that the teachers would arrive in their classrooms a few minutes late. Therefore, the stage was set. The students, 30 in each classroom, would execute the plan upon the entry of each class's teacher. Here's what happened…

What's Effective

 Teacher "A" entered her classroom ready to begin the day. Upon her entry, all of the students stood, turned their desks around, faced the back wall, and waited…. Teacher "A" responded immediately by taking her materials from her desk and bringing them to the back of the classroom. She then smiled and said, "Needed a change of scenery today? Me, too!" She then proceeded to teach for the rest of the class period from the "back" of the room. Instruction went on without skipping a beat! Not a word was said, but the looks on the faces of the students were priceless. It was a day neither Teacher "A" nor her students would ever forget.

What's *Not* Effective

Teacher "B" entered her classroom ready to begin the day. Upon her entry, all of the students stood, turned their desks around, faced the back wall, and waited... Teacher "B" responded immediately by crossing her arms, locking her stance, tightening her jaw, and saying, "All right—whose idea was it? Turn around, every one of you, right now!" One by one the students turned their desks around, careful not to make eye contact with their teacher. Two students began giggling and were quickly reprimanded and were dared to laugh again. After all, this was a serious offense and it would be treated in a serious manner! Again, the question came, but this time with more force: "Whose idea was it?" No one answered. "I'm not letting up. You *will* tell me who thought up this little scheme of yours. Now, I'm asking you again, whose idea was it?" Again, no response. "All right, if that's how you want to play, let's play. You will stay inside at recess today and as many days as it takes until someone admits to starting all of this. *And*, I'm going to call each of your parents tonight to tell them what you've done. That might make you think twice before you do something so ridiculous and utterly disrespectful again. I'm surprised at all of you—and very disappointed...." The "lecture" went on for over 20 minutes. The phone calls took hours. It was a day neither Teacher "B" nor her students would ever forget.

Bottom Line

The fact is that children will be children—shame on them! How dare they! Another fact is that adults will sometimes forget that they are adults and enter into futile power struggles with children over the fact that children are acting like children. You see, children "try the patience" of adults. In doing so they're actually trying to prove that they can control adults. Regrettably, many adults fall prey by failing to control their actions and reactions. The children win! They prove it! We're imposters! Are we? Well, that depends on whether we are able to control our actions and reactions with others. Effective teachers know that the second they "lose control," they *lose control*. Therefore, they remain in control of their professionalism by learning to control their actions and reactions with their students. There is actual scientific research to prove that if you light a small fire and then throw gasoline on it, your chances of putting out the fire decrease significantly. The fire will take control. The same research proves that if you light a small fire and do *not* add fuel to it, deprived of oxygen and combustibles, it will quickly die. So put your fuel back where it belongs—in your car's gasoline tank. You'll get much more mileage out of it that way!

> *That was great—I just can't wait*
> *To pass it on to others*
> *You won't believe what they'll perceive*
> *And pass on to another.*
>
> *Translations sway another way*
> *Thus changes are quite likely*
> *So down the road when it explodes*
> *I'll just retreat politely.*
>
> Elizabeth Breaux

Resisting the Urge to Gossip

Classroom Scenario

She was referred to, affectionately, as "The Daily Advocate," in reference to the local newspaper. She seemed to know everything…sometimes before it even happened! She was a great storyteller, mesmerizing her audiences with her attention to minute details. She was always amusing. But, above all, she was *dangerous*.

It was the teachers' first day of school. (The students would begin on the following day.) As the teachers sat in groups at tables in the library, the counselors handed out the dreaded "lists"—*class rosters*! And as though someone had just shouted, "Start your engines," she shifted into overdrive. She began scrutinizing everyone else's rosters to "forewarn" them of the impending doom, given the "bad eggs" that each had unfortunately inherited for the next nine months. She proceeded to give a short synopsis of each "bad egg's" history at the school, along with a history of each one's parents and their inabilities to properly rear their children.

Several of the teachers listened intently, actually asking specific questions. One, believe it or not, was even taking notes!

And here's what happened next. One teacher at the table stood abruptly and emphatically shouted, "Stop. Let's try something different this year.

Why don't we pretend that we were all given the opportunity to *choose* the students whom we wish to teach this year and that the rosters that we now hold in our hands are of students we have *chosen* to teach?" Everyone, of course, (except for "The Daily Advocate" who had just experienced the wind gushing out of her sail), gave half-hearted giggles but then agreed that this was a great idea.

What's Effective

 The teacher who made this startling suggestion should be awarded the Nobel Peace Prize! Imagine teaching from the first day of school with the mindset that we are teaching only those students we have chosen! Imagine accepting the fact that if not for the students, each and every one of the little "eggs," we would not have jobs! Imagine treating each student as an individual no better or worse than ourselves! Imagine providing each student with a clean slate! Imagine erasing *all* of the notes on our "gossip" slates and then throwing them away! If you can imagine it, then you can *do it*! The mind is a powerful thing!

What's *Not* Effective

 On the "surface" gossip is a sometimes amusing, intriguing, and seemingly harmless activity, but it can, and does, have devastating consequences. As adults we all know this to be true. In fact, we try to teach this "fact of life" to our students. So why do we assume that it does not apply to us, the teachers?

Unfortunately, few of us can honestly say that we have never participated in some type of gossip. For some reason it seems to thrive in the teaching profession, where its effects can be the most detrimental, especially when the "talk" concerns the students whom we teach.

If we expect the worst from our students based on what we've "heard," they will give us just that: their worst. Students truly do live up (or down) to our expectations of them.

Bottom Line

 The simple fact is that gossiping about *anyone* at *any time* is *not effective*. It is dangerous and harmful. It has *never* helped a single student or a single adult. In the classroom those who formulate preconceived notions based on hearsay and gossip are paving their own roads to failure. But more importantly, they're taking it upon themselves to pave their students' roads to failure. *Resist the urge to gossip!*

> "If you do not have personal problems, then you are not a person. If you allow your personal problems to spill over into the classroom, then you are not a professional."

Annette Breaux[*]

Being a Professional

Classroom Scenario

It was the end of another long school day and for Ms. Randall, it had not been a good day. First of all, she had been up all night with a sick child. Then there had been a traffic jam that had caused her to be late for a very important meeting before school. To make matters worse, her first period class had been less than enthusiastic about the lesson that she had spent hours planning. And all of this before 9:00 a.m.! Oh, the life of a teacher…

As the dismissal bell rang to end the day, she knew that she had dealt with all that she could physically and emotionally handle in one day. Little did she know that her professionalism would be tested just one last time before the last bus exited the campus.

As she walked her class to the bus area, a student ran past her and in his rush to get to the bus almost knocked her to the ground. That was all it took. Before he could apologize, she began screaming, and he retaliated with much disrespect. Mr. Jones, another teacher, happened to see this and immediately stopped the student, as Ms. Randall proceeded to the bus area. Mr. Jones reprimanded the student, explaining to him in a calm, yet firm, manner that his reaction to Ms. Randall had been disrespectful. Mr. Jones then instructed the student to go to Ms. Randall and apologize to her, which the student immediately proceeded to do.

---

* From Breaux, A.L. (2003). *101 "Answers" for new teachers and their mentors* (p. 105). Larchmont, NY: Eye On Education. Used with permission

The student walked directly toward Ms. Randall and, in a very apologetic and mild manner (he knew that Mr. Jones was watching him), said to Ms. Randall, "I'm sorry." Ms. Randall looked briefly at the child, gave a disapproving grimace, which seemed to say, "Yeah, right…sure you are," turned her nose up, and walked away from him. The student turned and looked at Mr. Jones, shrugging his shoulders as if to ask, "What good did that do?"

What's Effective

The appropriate, professional, and most effective way for Ms. Randall to have handled that situation would have been to simply "suck it up" one last time (way deep down from her toes, if necessary), muster up the biggest smile she could possibly *fake* at that moment, and accept that apology as though it meant more to her than anything else in the world! Just imagine how powerful a gesture that would have been for that student. She could have then gone home and simply taken it out on her husband, like any "professional" would do!

What's *Not* Effective

Although we can all empathize with the frustration of Ms. Randall, we also recognize that Ms. Randall (possibly unintentionally) had just modeled the exact opposite of what we want to instill in our students: the importance of treating others in a dignified and respectful manner, *no matter what*! This child had just been given the "OK" to be disrespectful and rude when "it suits you." Ms. Randall certainly did not mean to model such behavior, but she did so nonetheless. She allowed her frustrations to overtake her professionalism. Big mistake!

Students will watch, scrutinize, and mimic their teachers in every way. If you don't believe that, just ask your class one day if anyone would like to imitate you! They *will* volunteer, and they *will* surprise you with their accurate imitations! They notice everything!

Bottom Line

 As professionals we must act professionally at all times, even and especially when we don't *feel* like it. Sometimes that might mean simply putting big smiles on our faces and just *faking* it. Students don't know the difference; they do, however, know the difference between our words and our actions. The fact is that they hear nothing we say and *everything* that we do. Do the "professional" thing, always! The students are watching!

FACT: If we enjoy what we do, we become better. If we do not enjoy what we do, we become bitter.

Enjoying What You Do

Classroom Scenario

Mr. Simmons waited anxiously in the hall to greet his students with a teeth-bearing smile, the same he displayed every day. Across the hall Mrs. Carlton also stood at her door. However, no teeth, no smile, no hint of one iota of happiness living within…. The students in Mr. Simmons' class were always busy, always productive, always successful. The students in Mrs. Carlton's class were never busy, never productive, and rarely successful. The happiness in Mr. Simmons' class was palpable. The misery in Mrs. Carlton's class was also palpable. Oddly enough, both Mr. Simmons and Mrs. Carlton had entered teaching at the same time, 19 years ago. Both had taught in the same school for the past 19 years.

When speaking with coworkers, Mr. Simmons was always upbeat and optimistic. Even in the face of adversity, he readily accepted any and all challenges his students had to offer. Mrs. Carlton, on the other hand, was always downtrodden and negative. She was known to the rest of the faculty (though unbeknown to her) as "Clyde." "Clyde" was short for Clydesdale, and the nickname, according to legend, had its roots in the fact that students, teachers, parents, or administrators who had to deal with her always walked away feeling like they had been run over by a Clydesdale! It was rumored that she was once overheard saying that if it weren't for the darned kids, she might be able to get something accomplished…. (Minor detail: If it weren't for the "darned" kids, she wouldn't have a job!)

When asked to do almost anything related to school, Mr. Simmons was always eager to volunteer. Mrs. Carlton, however, often threatened to contact her attorney when asked to do anything she considered "above and beyond the call of duty." The contrast was remarkable. How could two people teach the same students in the same place and work with the same people for the same amount of time yet have such totally different outlooks? It happened. Regrettably, this "scenario" is all too common in far too many classrooms.

For 19 years Mr. Simmons had enjoyed every day of his teaching career. For 19 years Mrs. Carlton had been miserable in her chosen career. Aha! The key word here is "chosen."

What's Effective

At the risk of overstating the obvious, the fact is that one of the reasons Mr. Simmons was so successful in teaching was largely due to his actually "enjoying" teaching! You see, Mr. Simmons had made a decision, many years earlier, to teach. However, let's not forget that he continued to choose teaching, every day, for 19 years. He loved children and he loved teaching. If you asked Mr. Simmons about his "job," he would tell you that he was lucky enough to actually get *paid* for something he loved to do. Mrs. Carlton, on the other hand, would say that she didn't get paid enough for what they asked her to do! Speaking of Mrs. Carlton, read on...

What's *Not* Effective

Mrs. Carlton was not a victim of her job. She was not a victim of her students. Rather, she was a victim of herself! For whatever reason, she had never enjoyed teaching. There's no sin in that. Teaching just wasn't for her. The actual "sin" was in the fact that she continued to inflict her misery upon others by continuing to do something she did not enjoy. Worse yet, she was inflicting her misery upon children who were counting on her to lead them, to teach them, to inspire them, to show them the way. Every year, for 19 years, she failed to live up to the responsibilities she continued to accept by renewing her contract as a "teacher." Every year, she became more miserable. Every day, the students suffered.

Bottom Line

The fact is that, as teachers, we actually pick our jobs. We apply for them, we go through interviews, and we sign contracts saying that we will live up to the awesome responsibilities that we have chosen to accept. None of us, as teachers, are victims of our jobs. We freely choose teaching every day, every year. We are free at any time to choose another profession. If we enjoy what we do, we become better. If we do not enjoy what we do, we become bitter. There is no place for stagnant, bitter adults in our schools.

If we choose to teach, we must choose to love what we do, to give it our all, and to be advocates, not adversaries, of children. The children are counting on us. Let's not let them down.

Dealing with Others

The Golden Rule

Do unto others just as you
Would like for them to do unto you
Listen with care, but do not dare
To tell someone else what to do
Be gentle and kind, and soon you will find
That they'll be the same way with you.

Annette L. Breaux,
"No Adults Allowed"

FACT 1:   A parent's perception of a teacher hinges largely on the student's perception of the teacher.

FACT 2:   When a teacher approaches a parent in a professional, tactful manner, the chances for successful communication and cooperation increase a hundredfold!

FACT 3:   Even the angriest of parents will eventually run out of steam if the teacher remains calm.

Dealing with Parents

Classroom Scenario

According to rumor Michael had been born with glue on his hands. Everywhere he went, things mysteriously disappeared. And often times those things were stuck to Michael's hands. He had been accused of "stealing" in grades 1 through 5. And now he had entered the 6th grade. Mrs. "Gotcha" was his homeroom teacher. She not only knew of the rumors, but she continued to spread them, even before Michael ever entered her classroom. She was determined to play "Columbo" from the very first day. Therefore, Mrs. Gotcha became a self-appointed vigilante. She watched and waited, oh so patiently, knowing her patience would eventually "pay off."

Sure enough, it happened. Denise approached Mrs. Gotcha one afternoon reporting that Michael had stolen a calculator from her book sack. Several "eye witnesses" were willing to testify on behalf of Denise, yet none of them actually saw what had happened. Mrs. Gotcha immediately went into action. She had her victim, she had several eyewitness accounts, and she had the criminal—*got him*! She accused Michael, in front of his classmates, of stealing the calculator. Michael, of course, denied the accusations. She screamed at him, he screamed back, she screamed some more, and he screamed some more. The punishment was doled out and was quite extreme. But hey, he deserved it according to Mrs. Gotcha, who, by the way, was basing her verdict on circumstantial evidence.

The next day Michael's mother called for a conference with Mrs. Gotcha. Mrs. Gotcha was more than anxious to defend her verdict. Here's what happened:

Mother (storming into classroom): I want to talk to you about what you did to my son, Michael!

Mrs. Gotcha: What I did? I think we need to talk about what Michael did!

Mother: He said that you accused him of stealing—in front of everyone! And you never even listened to *his* side of the story!

Mrs. Gotcha: His side of the story? He had no "side." He stole Denise's calculator.

Mother: Do you have proof of that?

Mrs. Gotcha: Even if I did, you'd take up for him anyway, just like you're doing right now! Your son can do no wrong in your eyes!

Mother: I'll show you who's wrong. I'm taking this to the school board!

Mrs. Gotcha: Go ahead. Take it wherever you'd like. But when Michael ends up in jail in a few years, don't come blaming me!

Okay, so what really happened in the classroom? Did Michael steal the calculator? Who knows? What we do know, however, is that a similar situation occurred, involving Michael once again, in the classroom of Mrs. "**F**air **A**nd **C**onsummately **T**actful" (Mrs. FACT, for short!). Read on to find out how a similar situation rendered completely different results.

What's Effective

 We'll begin by going straight to the parent conference, where the details of what happened in the classroom will all be revealed. This time, however, the conference took place between Michael's mother and Mrs. FACT.

Mother (storming into the classroom): I want to talk to about what you did to my son, Michael!

Mrs. FACT (in a soft, calm, professional manner): Sure. I'll be happy to talk to you about Michael. What would you like to talk about?

Mother: You accused him of stealing!

Mrs. FACT: Is that what Michael told you?

Mother: You're darned right, he did. Now what do you have to say for yourself?

Mrs. FACT: Well, the first thing I'd like to say is that I admire your concern for your son. That says that you're a dedicated parent. And as a concerned teacher I just want you to know that even if we end up disagreeing today, I respect your concern as a parent. That says a lot about you.

Mother: Well.... Thank you.

Mrs. FACT: Before I explain, I'd like for you to read something Michael wrote. (She hands a piece of paper to his mother containing Michael's own admission that he did take the candy from Susan.)

Mother (reading the note in astonishment): Well, that little liar! He did not admit this to me.

Mrs. FACT: I'll explain what happened. Please feel free to stop me at any time if you have any questions. Yesterday, following the candy sale, Susan told me that Michael had taken her candy. This, of course, was Susan's story. So in all fairness to Michael, I talked to him privately, told him what Susan had said, and asked him to please write his account of what had happened. I left him alone to do this, and I thanked him in advance, telling him I respected the fact that I knew I could count on him to be honest, even if it meant an admission of guilt. And what you just read is what he wrote. So we decided that his punishment would involve three things: (1) he would return Susan's candy, (2) he would apologize to Susan, and (3) he would share with you what he had written. I guess he forgot to show you the note....

Mother: Well, I'm a little embarrassed. He definitely did not show me this note. If he had, I wouldn't be here. I'm really sorry about this.

Mrs. FACT: Please don't apologize. I'm so glad we got to meet. And I look forward to working together with you in the future to ensure that we continue to do what's best for Michael. Thanks so much for taking time out of your busy schedule to come and meet with me.

Okay, it goes without saying that this was an extremely professional and effective way to handle such a situation—both with Michael and with his mother. The teacher addressed the problem when it happened, she listened to both sides, and she dealt with the problem fairly and tactfully. Therefore, when Michael's mother arrived, Mrs. FACT was prepared to deal with her. Also notice that Mrs. FACT had a way of "defusing" Michael's angry mother. Even though there was "proof" that Michael had indeed taken the candy, the conference could have been a disaster had she returned Michael's mother's defensiveness with counter-defensiveness. Instead, she remained calm and professional throughout. The mother lost all defensiveness and the conference ended up being quite productive.

What's *Not* Effective

 Whether or not Michael was actually "guilty" in Mrs. Gotcha's class, the fact remains that the way she handled the situation was *not* effective. To begin with, she never really proved that Michael had stolen the calculator. What happened to "innocent until proven guilty?" But to make matters worse, she immediately took a defensive stance with Michael's mother. From that point, there was nowhere to go but downhill. She succeeded in making Michael feel victimized and in turning Michael's mother against her. Sadly, her chances of ever getting Michael "back" are slim.

Bottom Line

 The bottom line is that a calm, professional approach is the *only* way to deal with parents, with students, and with anyone else for that matter. When parents come to you in anger, allow them to speak. Listen to what they have to say. You'll learn a lot. Above all, *never* get defensive. Let them know that you appreciate the very fact that they care enough to come to school to discuss the issue. Thank them for their concern. Immediately, you will defuse the anger. Then, you can work cooperatively to solve whatever problems their children, your students, may have. Most importantly, remain "Fair And Consummately Tactful." It's a *fact* that a "Gotcha" attitude is counterproductive. Remember, the real Lieutenant Columbo seeks out only the *facts!*

> "I absolutely *love* this job! I want to get better at keeping the lines of communication open between teachers and administration. If teachers are unhappy with a new procedure, directive, or whatever, they need to come to me with a solution! If they only complain to others, I will never know that there is a problem. I can't fix something if I don't know that it is broken!"
>
> Jody Slaughter,
> Middle School Assistant Principal

Dealing with Administrators

Classroom Scenario

It was the first in-service day for the teachers. The students would arrive tomorrow. As always, this was a busy day. There was a lot to cover in little time.

The teachers assembled in the library. A packet of important papers was given to each teacher as the administrator began addressing the lengthy agenda. The dreaded "duty schedule" was, naturally, at the top of the list. The teachers eagerly flipped through the pages of the schedule, praying that the administration had been kinder to them this year than last!

Sighs of relief along with muffled grumbles of discontent could be heard throughout the library. "They gave me the cafeteria," said one obviously unhappy teacher. "I wonder how much food I'll be wearing to 5th period this year!" "I got the courtyard," said another. "Too hot in the summer and too cold in the winter." "I'm stuck in the restrooms again," barked a third. "Someone is obviously out to get me!" "I surely do wish that we could rotate duties instead of being assigned the same one for the duration of the year," said another. "We did that at another school, but we'll never see that here. It takes too much time to devise a duty schedule like that!"

Begrudgingly, all did report to and fulfill their daily duties. They also continued to criticize the manner in which the schedule was devised. None of them, remarkably, ever approached the administrator with a solution! They did, however, continue to blame the administration for not being more compassionate to the needs of the individual teachers. This attitude only served to breed discontent among others who had previously thought that they were perfectly happy! (Don't you hate it when that happens?) In spite of all the frustrations and complaints, the administrator was never made aware that there was a problem!

What's Effective

The teacher with the solution could have agreed to be the spokesperson. He could have approached the administrator as a liaison, bringing both the concerns and the solutions to the table. Any effective administrator knows that a happy faculty is a productive and effective faculty whose attitudes will ultimately spill over into the classrooms.

(If the administrator really wanted to please her faculty, she could just cancel duty for the rest of the year! Oh well, maybe in another life....)

What's *Not* Effective

Talking "behind the administrator's back" about frustrations concerning the duty schedule was simply that—talk! It was not productive in that nothing changed. The "talk" served only to deepen the frustrations and animosities that were soon to snowball into even bigger problems, some of which the teachers did not even know were problems until the "problem seekers" brought the problematic situations to the attention of those who initially thought that they were basically problem free! (And you just thought *you* had problems....)

Bottom Line

Communication can work wonders! When used appropriately, it keeps things running smoothly. Remember that just because we do voice our concerns to the appropriate people, we will not always get what we want. However, when we approach situations from an appropriate and professional standpoint, we then gain the opportunity to understand the reasoning behind the decisions. We may not always agree, but we can agree to disagree. That's what *true* professionals do. If there is a problem, they direct their efforts *not* toward griping about the problem but toward finding a solution. When they find a solution, they present it to their administrator in a professional way. It's really that simple.

> *FACT: On any given faculty, some teachers spend MOST of their energies griping about their administrators. When you consider the fact that most teachers spend, on average, more than 90% of their time in their classrooms AWAY from their administrators, it is a definite waste to focus so much energy on someone they don't spend much time with at all! Imagine if all of that energy were saved for use where it really counts—in the classroom!*

> *I took the easy road, and did what I knew was wrong*
> *But friends of mine were watching, who sang a different song*
> *They pulled me from the doldrums and slapped me in the face*
> *They helped me come to understand the error of my ways.*
> *So I took "the road less traveled," the one that spells success*
> *And realized that this one, too, created quite a mess*
> *For those who took the easy road threw roadblocks in my way*
> *They hate to see another win a game that they won't play.*
> *But play I did and win I have, and now I'm called (I've heard)*
> *"A professional," by those I trust, "in every sense of the word."*
>
> Elizabeth Breaux

Dealing with Difficult Co-Workers

Classroom Scenario

Mr. James was the consummate professional who had many years of experience dealing with "at-risk" students and had always managed to be extremely successful. He taught the most difficult groups of students, yet he seldom, if ever, had discipline problems. His students were successful (some for the first time in their lives). He had very high standards from which he seldom wavered. He believed in taking students from where they were and leading them toward where they needed to be. No excuses allowed. He made none for himself and accepted none from his students. He was highly respected by students, teachers, parents, and administrators. He was the kind of teacher that we all aspire to be.

Unfortunately, he found himself one day engaged in conversation with one of the proverbial "excuse makers." Mr. James realized that, after only a few minutes in conversation, this teacher had referred to herself as a "dumping ground" three times. She kept insisting that because of the nature of the class that she taught, her students were simply unmotivated and would never take the course seriously. She also explained to Mr. James that this was something that she had grown accustomed to, as she had also been a "dumping ground" at the school where she had previously taught. She went on to explain that she had made a "list" of all of the "bad students" in the school, and that almost every single one of them ended up in her class!

Wanting to make certain that this teacher not believe that he would ever "buy in" to such a philosophy, while at the same time not revealing to her what he really thought of her philosophy, was difficult. Doing the "right thing" in a situation like this is a tough call. What is the "right" thing to say? Should you say anything at all for fear of having your words misconstrued? Mr. James refrained from saying what he would have liked to say. (He was, in fact, appalled that anyone calling themselves a teacher would consider making a "bad kid" list, not to mention having the audacity to actually admit it!) He remembered his own professionalism, however, and calmly said, "I can honestly say that I don't share your sentiments. I love teaching, and I love all of my students. In fact, in all of my years of teaching, I've never taught a "bad" student. I'm sorry that your experience has not been the same. And speaking of students, please excuse me. I've got to get back to my classroom." Mrs. "Dumping Ground" was left standing defenseless, defeated, and defused, in the "nicest" of ways.

What's Effective

 As much as we may try, we cannot escape the wrath of the unprofessional "professionals" with whom we may work every day. (True professionals accept this as a fact of life, albeit a difficult one at best.) We all know them, we've all worked with them, and we can spot them from a mile away. They are the ones who are often very poor classroom managers, thereby setting themselves up to have many discipline problems. Because they cannot "manage" a classroom, they become quite adept at "managing" to blame the problems on the students, the administration, the parents, and other teachers. They are the ones who insist that they are given the "bad" kids every year! Actually, if it weren't for the "kids," they'd be darned good teachers!

Consider the fact that students/people are products of their environments. A child will behave according to what is accepted and expected by the teacher. A student who is functioning in a positive, successful manner in one class but not another is proof that he is functioning according to his environment, an environment wherein the *only* "difference" is the teacher.

Experienced professionals cringe at the thought of having to be in the company of those who behave unprofessionally. The most difficult part of engaging in conversations with these "less than professional" teachers is that we cannot tell them what we truly think of their behavior—and boy would we love to!

The fact is that it is never worth losing your professionalism with someone who is obviously not in this profession for the love of children to begin with. Therefore, what Mr. James did was effective. He did not "engage," he did not "enable," and he did not "agree." And he managed to do all of this in a professional manner. Rest assured that this teacher no longer sought Mr. James' opinions. His "street" was a "dead end."

What's *Not* Effective

Engaging in unprofessional behavior and stooping to the levels of unprofessional people is *not* effective. It simply adds fuel to their fires and lends credence to their lack of professionalism, at least in their minds.… Misery does love company, unfortunately, and people who are miserable in their job settings tend to enlist the support of others who feel the same. They are looking for justifications for their misery without having to look at themselves for answers. And every time another teacher "agrees" with what they say, their "victimization" is affirmed and the overall school environment becomes a little less professional, one teacher at a time.

Bottom Line

Acting in any way other than a professional way is not only ineffective, but harmful! In acting unprofessionally, we relinquish our abilities to truly make a difference. And in enabling others to play out their roles as victims, we demoralize the profession. Dealing with difficult co-workers in a professional manner may be the ultimate test of our own professionalism. Are you up to the challenge?

She said my name every day
She smiled a lot
She was always prepared
She showed me how
She let me try on my own
She helped me with everything
She complimented my accomplishments
She bragged about me to others
She thanked me
She cried on the last day of school
That was thirty years ago, and I have not forgotten…

Elizabeth Breaux

Conclusion

It is I, the teacher, who makes the difference in the classroom. As a teacher, I am a role model, an advocate of student success, an influential person in the life of every student I teach. In order to handle the challenges of the classroom effectively, I must be a master of myself—my attitudes, my feelings, my actions, my expectations, and my resolute determination to do whatever it takes to be the best that I can be. I am honored to call myself "teacher," and I take that responsibility very seriously. I know that the only way to be effective is to continue to learn and grow, to practice patience, to shower my students with love and acceptance, to open their eyes to their amazing potential, and to help to mold their innocent dreams into successful realities.

Each student is a unique, worthwhile individual. It is my job, in the classroom, every day, to make each of them feel worthy, loved, safe, special. Every child, regardless of the disguise, knows what he or she is not. It is my job to teach each child what he or she can be!

I cannot control what will happen to my students down the road of life—what paths they will take, what choices they will make. Within my control, however, are my actions and reactions with every student I teach. My success comes from finding worth within each and nurturing the beauty that often lies hidden beneath life's layers of protection.

No, I cannot control what will happen to my students down the road of life, but I can help to make their loads lighter, their memories fonder, their successes sweeter…

For I am a teacher.

I touch students' hearts.

I touch students' lives.

An Invitation for Your Comments

It has been our absolute pleasure to share this book with you. We eagerly invite your input, your suggestions, or any stories you would like to share for future editions of this book. Please feel free to contact us:

Annette Breaux

abreaux@eyeoneducation.com

Elizabeth Breaux

ebreaux@eyeoneducation.com

You may also contact the publisher at:

Sickles@eyeoneducation.com